博雅 21世纪内容语言融合（CLI）系列英语教材

国家社会科学基金项目"英语专业基础阶段内容依托式课程改革研究"成果
高等教育国家级教学成果奖获奖项目成果
辽宁省普通高等教育本科教学成果奖获奖项目成果

美 国 国 情
美国社会与文化
（第3版）

UNDERSTANDING THE USA SOCIETY AND CULTURE
(THIRD EDITION)

常俊跃 李莉莉 赵永青 主编

北京大学出版社
PEKING UNIVERSITY PRESS

图书在版编目(CIP)数据

美国国情. 美国社会与文化 / 常俊跃，李莉莉，赵永青主编. —3 版. —北京：北京大学出版社，2021.9
21 世纪内容语言融合（CLI）系列英语教材
ISBN 978-7-301-32331-1

Ⅰ. ①美… Ⅱ. ①常…②李…③赵… Ⅲ. ①英语 – 阅读教学 – 高等学校 – 教材②文化史 – 美国 Ⅳ. ① H319.37

中国版本图书馆 CIP 数据核字 (2021) 第 190993 号

书　　　名	美国国情：美国社会与文化（第3版） MEIGUO GUOQING: MEIGUO SHEHUI YU WENHUA (DI-SAN BAN)
著作责任者	常俊跃　李莉莉　赵永青　主编
责任编辑	刘文静　吴宇森
标准书号	ISBN 978-7-301-32331-1
出版发行	北京大学出版社
地　　　址	北京市海淀区成府路 205 号　100871
网　　　址	http://www.pup.cn　新浪微博：@ 北京大学出版社
电子邮箱	编辑部 pupwaiwen@pup.cn　总编室 zpup@pup.cn
电　　　话	邮购部 010-62752015　发行部 010-62750672　编辑部 010-62759634
印刷者	北京溢漾印刷有限公司
经销者	新华书店
	787 毫米 ×1092 毫米　16 开本　13.25 印张　300 千字 2009 年 9 月第 1 版　2016 年 5 月第 2 版 2021 年 9 月第 3 版　2024 年 7 月第 4 次印刷
定　　　价	49.00 元

未经许可，不得以任何方式复制或抄袭本书之部分或全部内容。
版权所有，侵权必究
举报电话：010-62752024　电子邮箱：fd@pup.cn
图书如有印装质量问题，请与出版部联系，电话：010-62756370

第3版前言

长期以来,"以语言技能训练为导向"(Skill-Oriented Instruction,SOI)的教学理念主导了我国高校外语专业教育,即通过开设语音、语法、基础英语、高级英语、听力、口语、阅读、写作、翻译等课程开展语言教学,帮助学生提高语言技能。该理念对强化学生的语言技能具有一定的积极作用,但也导致了学生知识面偏窄、思辨能力偏弱、综合素质偏低等问题。

为了探寻我国外语专业教育的新道路,大连外国语大学英语专业教研团队在北美内容依托教学理念(Content-Based Instruction,CBI)的启发下,于2006年开展了校级和省级"内容本位教学"改革项目,还于2007年、2012年和2017年开展了3次国家社会科学基金项目推进课程体系改革,对CBI在我国的应用进行了系统探索,为推出内容语言融合教育理念(Content and Language Integration,CLI)奠定了实践基础。

教研团队批判性地吸收了国外CBI、内容语言融合学习(Content and Language Integrated Learning,CLIL)、以英语为媒介的教学(English as a Medium of Instruction,EMI)、沉浸式教学(Immersion)等理念关注内容的优点,以我国外语教学背景下十几年内容依托课程改革实践为依托,提出了具有中国特色的内容语言融合教育理念,即将目标语用于教授、学习内容和语言这两个重点,达到多种教育目的的教育理念。其特点如下:

1. 教育目标 有别于诸多外语教学理念,CLI不局限于语言,而是包含知识、能力和素质培养三个方面的目标。知识目标包含专业知识、相关专业知识、跨学科知识;能力目标包含语言能力、认知能力、交际能力、思辨能力等;素质目标包含人生观、价值观、世界观、人文修养、国际视野、中国情怀、责任感、团队意识等。

2. 教学特点 有别于单纯训练语言的教学,CLI主要特点体现在:语言训练依托内容,内容教学依靠语言;语言内容融合教学,二者不再人为割裂。

3. 师生角色 有别于传统教学和学生中心理念对师生角色的期待,CLI是在充分发挥教师主导作用的同时发挥学生的主体作用。教师可以扮演讲授者、评估者、建议者、资源提供者、组织者、帮助者、咨询者,同时也不排斥教师的权威角色、控制者等角色。学生角色也更加多元,包括学习者、参与者、发起者、创新者、研究者、问题解决者,乃至追随者。

4. 教学材料 有别于我国传统的外语教科书,它具有多类型、多样化的特点,包括课本、音频资料、视频资料、网站资料、教学课件、学生作品等。整个教材内容具有连续性和系统性;每个单元的内容都围绕主题展开。

5. 教学侧重 教学过程中,教师根据教学阶段或教学内容的特点确定教学重点,或侧重语言知识教学,或侧重语言技能教学,或侧重专业知识教学,或在语言教学和内容教学中达成某种平衡。

6. 教学活动 教学活动不拘泥于某一种教法所规定的某几种技巧,倡导充分吸收各种教法促进语言学习、内容学习、素质培养,运用多种教学手段,通过问题驱动、输出驱动等方法调动学生主动学习;运用启发式、任务式、讨论式、结对子、小组活动、课堂展示、项目依托教学等行之有效的方法,活动与学科内容教学有机结合,提高学生的语言技能,激发学生的学习兴趣,培养学生的自主性和创造性,提升学生的思辨能力和综合素质。

7. 教学测评 测评吸收测试研究和评价研究的成果,包括形成性评价和终结性评价。形成性评价可以有小测验、课堂报告、角色扮演、小组活动、双人活动、项目、撰写论文、撰写研究报告、创意写作、创意改写、反馈性写作、制作张贴作品等;终结性评价可以包括传统的选择题等各种题型。

8. 互动性质 有别于传统教学中信息从教师向学生的单向传送,其课堂互动是在师生互动基础上的生生互动、生师互动及至师生与其他人员的互动。

9. 情感处理 重视对学生的人文关怀,主张教师关注学生的情感反应,教学中有必要有效处理影响学生学习的各种情感因素。

10. 母语作用 尊重外语环境下师生的母语优势并加以利用。不绝对禁止母语的使用。母语的使用取决于教学的需要,母语用于有效支持教育目标的达成。

11. 应对失误 认可失误是学生获得语言或知识内容不可避免的现象,对学生失误采取包容的态度。针对具体情况应对学生的失误,或不去干预,允许学生自我纠正,或有针对性地适时给予纠正。

12. 理论支撑 语言学理论支撑包括:语言是以文本或话语为基础的;语言的运用凭借各种技能的融合;语言具有目的性。学习理论支撑包括:当人们把语言当成获取信息的工具而不是目的时学习语言更成功,作为语言学习基础的一些内容比另外一些内容更有用;当教学关注学生的需求时学生的学习效果会更好;教学应该以学生以前的学习经历为基础。

在 CLI 教育理念指导下,依托 3 个国家社会科学基金项目,我们将《高等学校英语专业英语教学大纲》规定的语言技能课程(包括英语语音、英语语法、英语听力、英语口语、英语阅读、英语写作、基础英语、高级英语、英语视听说、英汉笔译、英汉口译等)和专业知识课程(包括英语国家概况、英国文学、美国文学、语言学概论、学术论文写作等)进行系统改革,逐步构建了全新的英语专业课程体系,包括八个系列的核心课程:

1. 综合英语课:美国文学经典作品、英国文学经典作品、世界文学经典作品、西方思想经典。依托美国、英国及其他国家的英语文学经典作品和西方思想经典的内容,提高学生综合运用英语的能力,丰富对英语文学及西方思想的认知,提高综合能力和综合素养。

2. 英语视听说:美国社会文化经典电影、英国社会文化经典电影、环球资讯、专题资讯。依托美、英社会文化经典电影、环球资讯、专题资讯内容,提高学生的英语听说能力,同时增加学生对相关国家社会文化的了解。

3. 英语口语课:功能英语交际、情景英语交际、英语演讲、英语辩论。依托人际交往的知识内容，提高学生的英语口语交际能力，增进对人际沟通的了解。

4. 英语写作课：段落写作、篇章写作、创意写作、学术英语写作。依托笔头交际的知识内容，提高学生的英语笔头表达能力。

5. 英汉互译课：英汉笔译、汉英笔译、交替传译、同声传译、专题口译。依托相关学科领域的知识内容，提高学生的英汉笔译、交传、同传、专题口译技能，增加学生对相关领域的了解。

6. 社会文化课：美国社会与文化、美国自然人文地理、美国历史文化、英国社会与文化、英国自然人文地理、英国历史文化、澳新加社会与文化、欧洲文化、中国文化、古希腊罗马神话、《圣经》与文化、跨文化交际。依托相关国家或区域的社会、文化、史地等知识，扩展学生的社会文化知识，增加学生专业知识的系统性，拓宽学生的国际视野，同时提高学生的英语能力。

7. 英语文学课：英语短篇小说、英语长篇小说、英语散文、英语戏剧、英语诗歌。依托各种体裁的优秀文学作品内容，强化学生对英语文学文本的阅读，提高学生的文学欣赏能力及语言表达能力，提升学生的文学素养。

8. 语言学课程：英语语言学、英语词汇学、语言与社会、语言与文化、语言与语用。依托英语语言学知识内容，帮助学生深入了解英语语言，增加对语言与社会、文化、语用关系的认识，同时提升学生的专业表达能力。

此外，每门课程均通过开展多种教学活动，服务于学生的综合能力和综合素质培养目标。

研究表明，CLI指导下的课程改革在学生的语音、词汇、语法、听力、口语、写作、交际、思辨、情感、专业知识等诸多方面产生了积极的教学效果，对学生的文学作品分析能力、创新能力、思辨能力及逻辑思维能力发展也大有裨益。

CLI教育理念一经推出，在国际、全国、区域研讨会及我国高校广泛交流，产生了广泛的积极影响。

1. CLI教育理念影响了教师的教育理念。随着教学研究成果的不断出现，越来越多的英语教师开始关注CLI教育理念及其指导下的改革，数以百计的教师积极参与CLI教育教学研讨与交流，国际关系学院、华中农业大学、黑龙江大学等高校领导积极与团队成员交流理念及课程建设经验，两百多所高校引介了改革的理念、课程建设理念及开发的课程，而且还结合本校实际开展了课程改革，取得了积极成果。

2. CLI教育教学研究成果影响数万学生。在CLI教育理念指导下开发了系列课程和教材，在北京大学出版社、上海外语教育出版社等出版社出版；推出的校级、省级和国家级教学研究成果开始发挥辐射作用，通过《外语教学与研究》《中国外语》等期刊发表的研究论文向同行汇报了改革遇到的问题及取得的进展；数以万计的师生使用了我们开发的教材，在提高语言技能的同时扩展专业知识，提高综合素质。改革成果在我国的英语专业教育中发挥着积极的作用。

该理念不仅得到一线教师的广泛支持，也得到了戴炜栋、王守仁、文秋芳等知名专家的高度肯定。蔡基刚教授认为其具有"导向性"作用。孙有中教授认为，该理念指导的教学改革"走在了全国的前列"。教育部高等学校外语专业教学指导委员会前主任委员戴炜栋曾表示,开发的课程值得推广。此外,该理念被作为教学要求写入《外国语言文学类教学质量国家标准》及《普通高等学校本科外国语言文学类专业教学指南(上):英语类专业教学指南》,用于指导全国的外语专业教育,对我国的外语教育及教育教学改革必将产生深远的影响。

《美国国情:美国社会与文化(第3版)》是CLI教育理念指导下英语专业核心必修课程"基础英语"所使用的教材。教材针对的学生群体是具有中学英语基础的大学生,适用于英语专业一、二年级学生,也适用于具有中学英语基础的非英语专业学生和英语爱好者。总体看来,本教材具备以下主要特色:

1. 遵循了全新的教学理念。经过几十年的快速发展,我国的英语教学已经出现了翻天覆地的变化。今天的英语学习者不再仅仅满足于单词、语法、句型等英语语言知识的学习,他们更希望读到地道的英语,在享受英语阅读乐趣的同时又能增长见识,开阔国际视野,了解英语国家,进而更好地运用英语与英语国家人民进行交流。本教材改变了"为学语言而学语言"的传统教材建设理念,在具有时代特色且被证明行之有效的内容语言融合教育理念指导下,改变了片面关注语言知识和语言技能而忽视内容学习的做法。教材依托学生密切关注的美国社会文化内容,结合社会文化内容组织学生进行语言交际活动,在语言交流中学习有意义的知识内容,既训练语言技能,又丰富相关知识,起到的是一箭双雕的作用。

2. 涉及了丰富的教学内容。为了满足学生身心发展的需要,本教材提供的材料贴近社会,贴近学生,生动鲜活,丰富多彩,具有时代气息。教材以美国社会文化为主线,涉及美国人的性格、价值观、宗教信仰、学校教育、政治政体、生活方式、风俗节日、大众传媒、文学艺术、体育竞技、音乐赏析等主题。一切围绕大学生感兴趣的话题组织教材内容,以期用年轻人喜闻乐见的好材料帮助他们获得比较系统的美国社会文化知识,引导学生在认识和了解美国社会文化的基础之上,加深对于自身中国文化的理解,提升中国文化主体意识;通过异域社会文化知识的教学拓宽学生的国际视野,培养学生对文化差异的敏感性、宽容性以及处理文化差异的灵活性,以适应日益广泛、深入的国际文化交流的需求。

3. 引进了真实的教学材料。英语教材是英语学习者英语语言输入和相关知识输入的重要渠道。本教材大量使用真实、地道的语言材料,为学生提供了高质量的语言输入。此外,为了使课文内容更加充实生动,易于学生理解接受,编者在课文中穿插了大量的插图、表格、照片等真实的视觉材料,表现手段活泼,形式多种多样,效果生动直观。

4. 设计了新颖的教材板块。本教材每一单元的主体内容均包括 Before You Read, Start to Read, After You Read 和 Read More 四大板块,不仅在结构上确立了学生的主体地位,而且系统的安排也方便教师借助教材有条不紊地开展教学活动。它改变了教师单纯灌输、学生被动接受的教学方式,促使学生积极思考、提问、探索、发现、批判,培养自主获得知识、发现问题和解决问题的能力。

5. 提供了有趣的训练活动。为了培养学生的语言技能和综合素质,本教材在关注英语语言知识训练和相关知识内容传授的基础上精心设计了生动多样的综合训练活动,例如头脑风暴、话题辩论、角色表演、主题陈述、故事编述等。多样化的活动打破了传统教材单调的训练程式,帮助教师设置真实的语言运用情境,组织富于挑战性的、具有意义的语言实践活动,培养学生语言综合运用能力。

6. 推荐了经典的学习材料。教材的另一特色在于它对教学内容的延伸和拓展。在每章的最后,编者向学生推荐经典的图书、电影、诗歌、歌曲等学习资料,这不仅有益于学生开阔视野,也使教材具有了弹性和开放性,方便不同院校、不同水平学生的使用。

7. 引进了先进的数码技术。采用"互联网+"技术,实现从纸质资源到立体化多媒体资源的立体呈现,学习者可利用移动设备上的二维码扫描软件在线收听相关录音。

本教材是我国英语专业综合英语课程改革的一项探索,凝聚了全体编写人员的艰苦努力。然而由于水平有限,本教材还存在疏漏和不足,希望老师和同学们能为我们提出宝贵意见和建议。您的指导和建议将是我们提高的动力。

编者
2020 年 11 月 28 日
于大连外国语大学

Contents

Unit 1 Understanding American Society and Culture / 1
    Text A   American Culture / 2
    Text B   Five Famous Symbols of American Culture / 8
    Text C   Moral Values in America / 11

Unit 2 The American Character (I) / 15
    Text A   The American Character / 16
    Text B   What Is an American? / 19
    Text C   What Is Typically American? / 21

Unit 3 The American Character (II) / 25
    Text A   Typical American Behaviors and Values / 26
    Text B   Go-Go Americans / 31
    Text C   Time Is Money / 34

Unit 4 Religion in the U.S. / 37
    Text A   Religion in the United States / 38
    Text B   Puritanism / 44
    Text C   Community Hero: Millard and Linda Fuller / 46

Unit 5 The Mythical American West / 50
    Text A   The Impact of the American Frontier / 51
    Text B   Rugged Individuals / 58

Unit 6 Education in the U.S. / 61
    Text A   Education in the U.S. / 62
    Text B   The First Day of Middle School / 69

Text C   The Higher Learning in America: External Conditions / 71

Unit 7   Government and Politics in the U.S. / 77
Text A   The Organization of the American Government / 78
Text B   Why Not a Parliament? / 85
Text C   The Triumph of Technology / 87

Unit 8   The U.S.—A Nation of Nations / 91
Text A   The U.S.—A Nation of Nations / 92
Text B   The History of Chinese Americans / 98
Text C   African-American / 100

Unit 9   Love and Marriage in the U.S. / 104
Text A   Marriage: American Style / 105
Text B   Wedding Customs & Superstitions / 110
Text C   Dating Patterns / 113

Unit 10   Family Life in the U.S. / 117
Text A   American Family / 118
Text B   Divorce / 123
Text C   Decay of Family Relationships / 124

Unit 11   Holidays and Festivals in the U.S. / 129
Text A   The Winter Holiday Season / 130
Text B   American Vacations / 136
Text C   American Holidays / 138

Unit 12   Sports in the U.S. / 142
Text A   Sports in the U.S. / 143
Text B   All-American Football / 149
Text C   Air Jordan Walks Away / 150

Unit 13   The Charm of American Screens / 154
Text A   Entertainment Media in the U.S. / 155
Text B   Hollywood: How the American Movie Industry Was Born / 161
Text C   American Soap Operas / 163
Text D   Oprah Winfrey / 164

Unit 14 The Music of America / 169
    Text A   The Music of America / 170
    Text B   The King of Rock 'n' Roll / 176
    Text C   Jazz / 178

Unit 15 American Literature / 182
    Text A   Overview of American Literature / 183
    Text B   Man Is Not Made for Defeat / 189
    Text C   The Tempest / 191
    Text D   How to Read Stories / 193

重点参考书目和网站 / 198

Unit 1
Understanding American Society and Culture

> In a low-context culture, very little is taken for granted. Whilst this means that more explanation is needed, it also means there is less chance of misunderstanding particularly when visitors are present.
> —Edward T. Hall

Unit Goals

- To gain a general knowledge of American society and culture
- To adopt a right attitude towards cultural differences
- To get acquainted with some basic cultural concepts concerning American society and culture
- To develop critical thinking and intercultural communication skills
- To learn useful words and expressions about American society and culture and improve English language skills

Before You Read

Test your knowledge about American culture.
1. When people talk about the U.S. as a nation of immigrants, you may think of the nickname _____.
2. When people talk about freedom, you may think of the Statue of _____ in New York.
3. When people talk about going to the U.S. to pursue success, you may say they want to achieve their _____.
4. When people talk about the Civil Rights Movement in the U.S., you may think of the leader _____ and his speech _____.

5. When people talk about popular American sport, you may think of the ball game _____.
6. When people talk about Thanksgiving in the U.S., you know the bird served on the dinner table is likely to be _____.

Start to Read

Text A   American Culture

1. American culture is of Western culture in general. Having been developing since long before the United States became a country, it gradually obtains its own unique **characteristics** as is reflected in its dialect, music, arts, cuisine, etc. Today the United States of America is a **diverse** and **multi-cultural** country as a result of mass scale **immigration** from many countries.

The Culture out of Many

2. In general, Americans come in all different colors and **nationalities**. Americans practice different religions, and live many different lifestyles. Important differences exist between geographical regions, between rural and urban areas, and between social classes. In addition, the presence of millions of immigrants who came to the United States from all corners of the world with their own culture and values adds even more **variety** and flavor to American life.

3. Because of its **colonial** ties with the British, early American culture was

chiefly influenced by British culture. Other European cultures influenced American culture as well, **prominently** those of Ireland, Germany and countries from which large numbers of **immigrants** came. Influences also came from Latin America, Asia, and Africa, especially the western part of Africa from which the ancestors of most African Americans came. American culture also shares some features with the cultures of its neighbors in the New World.

4. The United States has been traditionally known as a melting pot, but recent developments reveal the characteristics of cultural **diversity** and **pluralism**, presenting the image of a salad bowl rather than a melting pot. In American culture, there are many **integrated** but unique **subcultures** which are connected with social classes, political **orientations** and a **multitude** of demographic characteristics such as ancestral traditions, sex and sexual orientation, making American culture **heterogeneous**.

The Culture of Its Own

5. Although Americans do not always agree with each other, they are **united** by a very special thing: the values and ideals that were originally described in the U. S. Constitution over 200 years ago. Probably above everything else, Americans consider themselves individuals. There are strong family ties and strong **loyalties** to groups, but **individuality** and individual rights are most important. If this seems like a selfish attitude, it also leads Americans to an honest respect for other individuals and an **insistence** on human **equality**.

6. Related to this respect for individuality are American traits of independence and **self-reliance**. From an early age, children are taught to "stand on their own two feet," an idiom meaning to be independent. Honesty and **frankness** are two more aspects of American individuality, and they are more important to Americans than personal honor or "saving face."

7. Americans place a high value on achievement and this leads them to constantly **compete** against each other. You will find friendly, and not-so-friendly, competition everywhere. Americans can also be **obsessed** with records of achievement in sports, in business, or even in more **mundane** things. On the other hand, even if Americans are often competitive, they also have a good sense of **teamwork** and of cooperating with others to achieve a specific goal.

8. Americans are often accused of being **materialistic** and driven to succeed. How much money a person has, how much profit a business deal makes, or how many material goods an individual **accumulates** is often their definition of success. This goes back to American competitiveness. Many Americans,

however, do not agree with this **definition** of success; they enjoy life's simple pleasures and are neither overly ambitious nor **aggressive**. Many Americans are materially successful and still have time to appreciate the cultural, spiritual, and human aspects of life.

After You Read

Knowledge Focus

1. Write T if the statement is true and F if it is false according to the cultural knowledge presented above.

   1) The United States has traditionally been known as a melting pot, but nowadays people prefer to call the nation a salad bowl. _____
   2) The strongest influences on American culture came from Southern European cultures. _____
   3) There are great regional and subcultural differences, making American culture mostly homogeneous. _____
   4) American people value family or group interests more than anything else. _____
   5) To American people, "face" is more important than honesty. _____
   6) Americans are often competitive, and they do not have a good sense of teamwork. _____

2. Pair work: Work with your partner and consider the following questions.

   1) What aspects of America that attract immigrants from different parts of the world?
   2) What could the U.S. gain from its immigrants?
   3) How do you understand "individuality"? Is this value acceptable to you?
   4) What is your definition of success? Share your ideas with your partner.

Language Focus

1. Build your vocabulary.

   A. Write the correct word next to its definition.

accumulate	obsess	prominent	insistence
heterogeneous	variety	integrate	compete

   _____ to measure oneself against others

   _____ conspicuous in position or importance

   _____ make into a whole

   _____ be preoccupied with something

   _____ continual and persistent demands

_____ a collection containing different sorts of things
_____ to increase gradually in quantity or number
_____ consisting of elements that are not of the same kind or nature

B. Use the proper forms of the words to complete the sentences.
1) The fear of death _____ her throughout her old age.
2) By investing wisely she _____ a fortune.
3) His lecture ranged over a _____ of topics.
4) Things have changed. What's the point of _____ on the rotten rules?
5) A popular culture is a large _____ group, often highly individualistic and constantly changing.
6) He is a _____ scholar in the field of linguistics.
7) Our school _____ against many other schools in baseball.
8) This is an important measure to _____ science and technology with economy.

2. **Fill in the blanks with the proper forms of the words.**
   1) The oldest son will _____ (inheritance) the title.
   2) When boundaries between countries are not clearly _____ (definition), there is usually trouble.
   3) Nobody can entirely keep away from this _____ (compete) world.
   4) I may say in all sincerity that you have been my most _____ (loyalty) friend.
   5) We should get a thorough understanding about the cultural _____ (diverse) of the United States.
   6) A _____ (frankness) discussion can help to clear the air.
   7) Ambition is a _____ (character) of all successful businessmen.
   8) A good salesman must be _____ (aggress) if he wants to succeed.

3. **Fill in each blank with a suitable preposition or adverb.**
   1) Americans come _____ all different colors and nationalities.
   2) Millions of immigrants came to the United States from all corners of the world _____ their own culture and values.
   3) Although Americans do not always agree _____ each other, they are united by a very special thing.
   4) Probably _____ everything else, Americans consider themselves individuals.
   5) There are strong family ties and strong loyalties _____ groups, but individuality and individual rights are most important.
   6) Individuality also leads Americans to an honest respect _____ other individuals and an insistence _____ human equality.
   7) Americans place a high value _____ achievement and this leads them to constantly compete _____ each other.

8) Americans can also be obsessed _____ records of achievement in sports, in business, or even in more mundane things.

9) Americans also have a good sense of teamwork and of cooperating _____ others to achieve a specific goal.

10) Americans are often accused _____ being materialistic and driven to succeed.

4. **Proofreading and error correction.**

The passage contains FIVE errors. Each indicated line contains a maximum of ONE error. In each case, only ONE word is involved. You should proofread the passage and correct it in the following way:

For a wrong word, underline the wrong word and write the correct one in the blank provided at the end of the line.

For a missing word, mark the position of the missing word with a "∧" sign and write the word you believe to be missing in the blank provided at the end of the line.

For an unnecessary word, cross the unnecessary word and put the word in the blank provided at the end of the line.

We recognize that there are expectations concerning "culture" that must also met. Certainly, we have tried for a balanced vision of facets of "high culture," include the arts, sciences and academic studies, "mass culture," associate with mass media and consumption, and the more difficult question of "popular culture." In all these areas, we have concerned to discuss not only the phenomena themselves, and questions of ideology and imagery.	1) _____ 2) _____ 3) _____ 4) _____ 5) _____

Comprehensive Work

1. **Talk about the differences between American culture and Chinese culture.**

1) Have you detected any major differences between the American and the Chinese? You may make reference to the following pictures and talk about the differences with your partners.

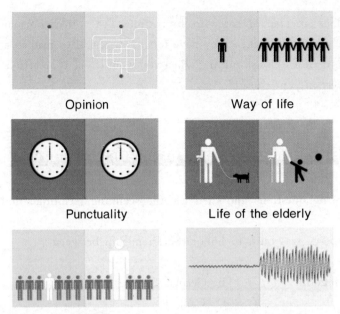

Opinion   Way of life

Punctuality   Life of the elderly

The boss   In the restaurant

2) Can you think of any other cultural differences between the American and the Chinese besides the differences illustrated above?
3) What do you think is the right attitude towards cultural differences?

2. Essay Writing.

Do you know any friends or persons from the United States? How do they impress you? Write about the most impressive and share your writing with your classmates.

Read More

> #### Scanning and Skimming
>
> **Scanning** is a technique you often use when looking up a word in the telephone book or dictionary. You search for key words or ideas. In most cases, you know what you are looking for, so you are concentrating on finding a particular answer. Scanning involves moving your eyes quickly down the page seeking specific words and phrases. Scanning is also used when you first find a resource to determine whether it will answer your questions. Once you have scanned the document, you might go back and skim it.
>
> **Skimming** is used to quickly identify the main ideas of a text. When you read the newspaper, you are probably not reading it word by word.

Skimming is done at a speed three to four times faster than normal reading. People often skim when they have lots of materials to read in a limited amount of time. Use skimming when you want to see if an article may be of interest in your research.

Text B Five Famous Symbols of American Culture

1. **First read the following questions and then use the scanning technique to find the answers.**

   1) The Statue of Liberty was built to honor the friendship between _____ and the United States.
      A. the United Kingdom   B. Germany
      C. France   D. Canada

   2) Which of the following statements about Barbie is NOT true?
      A. The original model for Barbie was a German doll and it was actually a joke gift for adults.
      B. Since her introduction in 1959, Barbie has become very popular in the U.S.
      C. Barbie's boyfriend, Ken, was introduced in 1961 and named after Barbara's brother.
      D. The Handlers are all very pleased with the Barbie doll.

   3) The painting *American Gothic* is an often-copied interpretation of the solemn pride of American _____.
      A. bankers   B. farmers
      C. clergymen   D. workers

   4) The most enduring portrait of Uncle Sam actually resembles _____.
      A. Sam Wilson   B. Brother Jonathan
      C. James Flagg   D. Grant Wood

2. **Fill in the blanks with proper prepositions after careful reading of the text.**

   1) Frederic Auguste Bartholdi was working _____ an enormous project called Liberty Enlightening the World.

   2) Ruth came up _____ the idea for Barbie after watching her daughter play with paper dolls.

   3) While white people had previously been used as models _____ most American coins, famed artist James Earle Fraser went _____ tradition by using three actual American Indians as models for his creation.

   4) Nan later remarked that the fame she gained from *American Gothic* saved her _____ a very boring life.

The Statue of Liberty

In the mid-1870s, French artist Frederic Auguste Bartholdi was working on an enormous project called Liberty Enlightening the World, a monument celebrating the U.S. independence and the France-America alliance. At the same time, he was in love with a woman whom he had met in Canada. His mother could not approve of her son's affection for a woman she had never met, but Bartholdi went ahead and married his love in 1876.

That same year, Bartholdi had assembled the statue's right arm and torch, and displayed them in Philadelphia. It is said that he had used his wife's arm as the model, but felt her face was too beautiful for the statue. He needed someone whose face represented suffering yet strength, someone more severe than beautiful. He chose his mother.

The Statue of Liberty was dedicated on an island in Upper New York Bay in 1886. It had his mother's face and his wife's body, but Bartholdi called it "my daughter, Liberty."

Barbie

Before all the different types of Barbie dolls for sale now, there was just a single Barbie. Actually, her name was Barbara. Barbara Handler was the daughter of Elliot and Ruth Handler, co-founders of the Mattel Toy Company. Ruth came up with the idea for Barbie after watching her daughter play with paper dolls.

The three-dimensional model for Barbie was a German doll—a joke gift for adults described as having the appearance of "a woman who sold sex." Mattel refashioned the doll into a decent, all-American version—although with an exaggerated breast size—and named it after Barbara, who was then a teenager.

Since her introduction in 1959, Barbie has become the universally recognized Queen of the Dolls. Mattel says that an average American girl owns ten Barbie dolls, and two are sold somewhere in the world every second.

Now more than sixty years old, Barbara, who declines interviews but is said to have loved the doll, may be the most famous unknown figure on the planet. Barbie's boyfriend, Ken, was introduced in 1961 and named after Barbara's brother. The real Ken, who died in 1994, was disgusted by the doll that made his family famous. "I don't want my children to play with it," he said in 1993.

American Gothic

Grant Wood instantly rose to fame in 1930 with his painting *American Gothic*, an often-copied interpretation of the solemn pride of American farmers. The painting shows a serious-looking man and a woman standing in front of a farmhouse. He was strongly influenced by medieval artists and inspired by the Gothic window of an old farmhouse, but the faces in his composition were what captured the world's attention.

Wood liked to paint faces he knew well. For the grave farmer, he used his dentist, a sour-looking man. For the woman standing alongside him, the artist chose his sister, Nan. He stretched the models' necks a bit, but there was no doubt they posed for the portrait. Nan later remarked that the fame she gained from *American Gothic* saved her from a very boring life.

The Buffalo Nickel

Today, American coins honor prominent figures of the U. S. government—mostly famous former presidents. But the Buffalo nickel, produced from 1913 to 1938, honored a pair of connected tragedies from the settlement of the American frontier—the destruction of the buffalo herds and the American Indians.

While white people had previously been used as models for most American coins, famed artist James Earle Fraser went against tradition by using three actual American Indians as models for his creation. For the buffalo on the other side, Fraser was forced to sketch an aging buffalo from New York City's Central Park Zoo since buffalo no longer wandered about the great grasslands. Two years later, in 1915, this animal was sold for $100 and killed for meat, a hide, and a wall decoration made from its horns.

Uncle Sam

Fourteen-year-old Sam Wilson ran away from home to join his father and older brothers in the fight to liberate the American colonies from the British during the American Revolution. At age 23, he started a meatpacking business and earned a reputation for being honest and hard-working.

During a later war in 1812, Wilson gained a position inspecting meat for U.S. Army forces, working with a man who had signed a contract with the government to provide meat to the army. Barrels of meat supplied to the army were stamped "EA-US" identifying the company (EA) and country of origin (U.S.). According to one story, when a government official visited the plant and asked about the letters, a creative employee told him that US was short for "Uncle Sam" Wilson. Soon soldiers were saying all Army supplies were from "Uncle Sam."

After the war, a character called Uncle Sam began appearing in political cartoons, his form evolving from an earlier cartoon character called Brother Jonathan that was popular during the American Revolution. Uncle Sam soon replaced Brother Jonathan as America's most popular symbol. The most enduring portrait of Uncle Sam was created by artist James Montgomery Flagg in his famous army recruiting posters of World Wars I and II. That version—a tall man with white hair and a small white beard on his chin, a dark blue coat and a tall hat with stars on it—was a self-portrait of Flagg.

Text C Moral Values in America

1. **First read the following questions and then use the scanning technique to find the answers.**

    1) Americans still believe that "honesty is the best policy." The well-known legend about _____ and the cherry tree teaches this value clearly.
        A. Abraham Lincoln   B. George Washington   C. Thomas Jefferson
    2) "The Rabbit and the Turtle" is a story from Aesop's fable, which teaches the virtue of _____.
        A. modesty   B. tolerance   C. perseverance
    3) The story of "The Good Samaritan" from the *Bible* describes a man who showed _____.
        A. compassion   B. responsibility   C. affection

2. Moral values in America are like those in any culture. In fact, many aspects of morality are universal. Can you find some Chinese stories and traditions that teach similar moral values?

Do Americans have any morals? That's a good question. Many people insist that ideas about right and wrong are merely personal opinions. Some voices are calling Americans back to traditional moral values. William J. Bennett, former U. S. Secretary of Education, edited *The Book of Virtues* in 1993 to do just that. Bennett suggests that great moral stories can build character. The success of Bennett's book shows that many Americans still believe in moral values. But what are they?

To begin with, moral values in America are like those in any culture. But the stories and traditions that teach them are unique to each culture. Not only that, culture influences how people show these virtues.

One of the most basic moral values for Americans is honesty. The well-known legend about George Washington and the cherry tree teaches this value clearly. Little George cut down his father's favorite cherry tree while trying out his new hatchet. When his father asked him about it, George said: "I cannot tell a lie. I did it with my hatchet." Instead of  punishment, George received praise for telling the truth. Sometimes American honesty—being open and direct—can offend people. But Americans still believe that "honesty is the best policy."

Another virtue Americans respect is perseverance. Remember Aesop's fable about the turtle and the rabbit that had a race? The rabbit thought he could win easily, so he took a nap. But the turtle finally won because he did

not give up. Another story tells of a little train that had to climb a steep hill. The hill was so steep that the little train had a hard time trying to get over it. But the train just kept pulling all the while saying: "I think I can, I think I can." At last, the train was over the top of the hill. "I thought I could, I thought I could," chugged the happy little train.

Compassion may be the queen of American virtues. The story of "The

Good Samaritan" from the *Bible* describes a man who showed compassion. On his way to a certain city, a Samaritan man found a poor traveler lying on the road. The traveler had been beaten and robbed. The kind Samaritan, instead of just passing by, stopped to help this person in need. Compassion can even turn into a positive cycle. In the fall of 1992, people in Iowa sent truckloads of water to help Floridians hit by a hurricane. The next summer, during the Midwest flooding, Florida returned the favor. In less dramatic ways, millions of Americans are quietly passing along the kindnesses shown to them.

In no way can this brief description cover all the moral values honored by Americans. Courage, responsibility, loyalty, gratitude and many others could be discussed. In fact, Bennett's bestseller—over 800 pages—highlights just 10 virtues. Even Bennett admits that he has only scratched the surface. But no matter how long or short the list, moral values are invaluable. They are the foundation of American culture.

Notes

1. **Edward T. Hall** (1914—2009) is a respected anthropologist and cross-cultural researcher. He received his Ph.D. from Columbia University in 1942 and continued field work and direct experience throughout Europe, the Middle East and Asia. During the 1950s he worked for the United States State Department teaching inter-cultural communications skills to foreign service personnel, developed the concept of "high context culture" and "low context culture," and wrote several popular practical books on dealing with cross-cultural issues, such as *The Silent Language*, *The Hidden Dimension*, *Beyond Culture*, etc.

2. **George Washington** (1732—1799) was the commander of the Continental Army in the American Revolutionary War (1775—1783) and served as the first President of the United States of America (1789—1797). Washington is seen as a symbol of the United States and republicanism in practice. His devotion to civic virtue made him an exemplary figure among early American politicians. Washington died in 1799, and the funeral oration delivered by Henry Lee stated that, of all Americans, he was "first in war, first in peace, and first in the hearts of his countrymen." Washington has been consistently ranked by scholars as one of the greatest U.S. Presidents.

For Fun

Books to Read

Jim Cullen: *American Dream*

    A short history of an idea that shaped the United States of America.

Richard Rorty: *Achieving Our Country*

    A collection of lectures on the Leftist thought in the twentieth-century America.

Movies to See

The Gua Sha Treatment

    A story of cross-cultural conflict which resulted from an age-old Chinese skin-scraping method *Gua Sha*.

The Joy Luck Club

    The life histories of four Chinese women and their relationships with their daughters who were born in the United States.

Unit 2
The American Character (I)

> We hold these truths to be self-evident, that all men are created equal, that they are endowed by their Creator with certain inalienable rights, that among these are Life, Liberty and the pursuit of Happiness.
> —The *Declaration of Independence*

Unit Goals

- To understand basic values and beliefs of American people
- To learn some cultural concepts concerning American character
- To develop critical thinking and intercultural communication skills
- To learn useful words and expressions that describe American character and improve English language skills

Before You Read

1. **Build your vocabulary.**

   Read the quotation from the *Declaration of Independence* at the beginning of the unit, and find the words with the following meanings. Write the word next to its meaning.

   _____ the act of trying to achieve something in a determined way

   _____ easily noticed or understood; obvious

   _____ that cannot be taken away from you

   _____ given a good quality

2. Pick out three qualities you associate most with Americans.

energetic	honest	industrious	sophisticated	intelligent
friendly	greedy	inventive	rude	adventurous
extroverted	introverted	fast-paced	out-going	modest
reserved	self-reliant	aggressive	materialistic	romantic
optimistic				

This is the typical American in my eyes:

_____

Start to Read

Text A　The American Character

1. What do Americans believe in? What is the American character? These questions are hard to answer, because there are so many Americans and they believe in so many different things. However, the history of the United States does provide some understanding of certain basic **characteristics** that many Americans share.

2. One of the main reasons why the early settlers came to America was to escape the controls they had experienced in Europe. There, small groups of wealthy people prevented them from moving into a higher social position or becoming wealthy, and government-supported churches controlled their **religious** practices and beliefs. Because these early settlers wanted to be free from such controls, they brought to America the view that the individual was **supremely** important. The settlers were against the efforts of the church, the society, and particularly the government, to control their actions. These controls came to be viewed as "un-American."

3. This strong American belief in **individualism** has both **positive** and **negative** sides. On the positive side, it has **strengthened** Americans' inventiveness and their belief in hard work. On the negative side, the belief in individualism has sometimes prevented Americans from using their government to solve their common problems. Americans prefer not to have government solutions to social problems.

4. The belief in individualism is a basic part of American character. This belief has at least two separate parts—**idealism** and **materialism**. Although these two beliefs are quite different, most Americans try to live with them both at the same time. And idealism and materialism are both very much a part of the American character.

5. American idealism comes largely from the nation's **Protestant** religious **heritage**. Early Americans did not have to belong to any particular church to have this belief. It influenced all Americans so strongly that idealism came to mean that each individual should possess a high moral character, and should live by his or her own beliefs. This is what American idealism means today.

6. Americans also have a strong belief in materialism, that is, each individual should gain as much wealth as possible. The American belief in materialism is partly a result of the nation's great material **abundance**. The early settlers found a continent with great forests, rivers, and **fertile** farmland in abundance.

7. As the United States grew and developed, the supply of natural resources seemed endless. Each generation had a chance to become wealthier than their parents had been. Americans **eventually** developed the belief that it was almost a duty to get rich.

After You Read

Knowledge Focus

1. **Write down the main points outlined in Text A.**
   American people have a strong belief in ___A___,
   which has both ___B___ and ___C___ aspects;
   in addition, ___A___ can be sub-divided into two separate parts:

   ```
         / \
       D     E
   ```

   ___D___ is closely related to protestant belief, while ___E___ encourages each individual to gain as much wealth as possible.

   ___A___, ___B___, ___C___, ___D___ and ___E___ refer to _____, _____, _____, _____ and _____.

2. Discuss with your partner and answer the following questions.
   1) Why did early settlers emigrate from Europe to America?
   2) What does American idealism mean? What is the major cause of this belief?
   3) What has produced American materialism?

3. Write T if the statement is true and F if it is false.
   1) As a nation of enormous diversity, the United States of America does not have a national identity. _____
   2) Early settlers came to America for individual freedom. _____
   3) American idealism makes material wealth undesirable. _____
   4) Protestant belief of the American people demands their great respect to the churches. _____
   5) The American belief in materialism partly results from the great material abundance of the U.S. _____

Language Focus

1. These are the 10 key words in Text A. Discuss their meanings with your partner.

characteristics	individualism	positive	negative
strengthen	inventiveness	idealism	materialism
heritage	abundance		

2. Work with a partner and answer the following questions.
   1) What do you think are the basic characteristics Americans share?
   2) Does a person believing in individualism like being helped all the time?
   3) What are the positive and negative sides of this Americans' strong belief in individualism?
   4) Is China a country of great material abundance?
   5) Would a person believing in materialism prefer to own many possessions or few?

3. Fill in each blank with a suitable preposition.
   1) What do Americans believe _____?
   2) These early settlers wanted to be free _____ such controls.
   3) Americans prefer not to have government solutions _____ social problems.
   4) Early Americans did not have to belong _____ any particular church to have this belief.
   5) Each individual should live _____ his or her own beliefs.
   6) The early settlers found a continent _____ great forests, rivers, and fertile farmland _____ abundance.

4. **Proofreading and error correction.**

   The passage contains FOUR errors. Each indicated line contains a maximum of ONE error. In each case, only ONE word is involved.

For Adams, a theme was more important than what he called that American dream of a better, richer, and happy life for all our citizens of every rank. That dream or hope has been present from the start. Ever since we become an independent nation, each generation has seen an uprising of an ordinary American to save that dream from the forces appeared to be overwhelming it.	1) _____ 2) _____ 3) _____ 4) _____

Comprehensive Work

1. **Work in group of four and share ideas with your group members.**

   Americans believe strongly in self-reliance and independence of the individual. What are the advantages and disadvantages of being very independent? Which is more important to you, pleasing your family or having the freedom to do what you want?

2. **Essay Writing.**

   Do you think wealth and possessions make a person important? If not, what does?

Read More

Text B　**What Is an American?**

By Bradford Smith

Americans are a peculiar people. They work like mad, then give away much of what they earn. They play until they are exhausted, and call this a vacation. They love to think of themselves as tough-minded business men, yet they are pushovers for any hard luck story. They have the biggest of nearly everything including government, motor cars and debts, yet they are afraid of bigness. They are always trying to chip away at big government, big business, big unions, big influence.

They like to think of themselves as little people, average men, and they would like to cut everything down to their own size. Yet they boast of their tall buildings, high mountains, long rivers, big state, the best country, the best world, the best heaven. They also have the most traffic deaths, the most waste, the most racketeering.

When they meet, they are always telling each other, "Take it easy," then they rush off like crazy in opposite directions. They play games as if they were fighting a war, and fight wars as if playing a game. They marry more, go broke more often and make more money than any other people. They love children, animals, gadgets, mother, work, excitement, noise, nature, television shows, comedy, installment buying, fast motion, spectator sports, the underdog, the flag, Christmas, jazz, shapely women and muscular men, classical recordings, crowds, comics, cigarettes, warm houses in winter and cool ones in summer, thick beefsteaks, coffee, ice cream, informal dress, plenty of running water, do-it-yourself, and a working week trimmed to forty hours or less.

They crowd their highways with cars while complaining about the traffic, flock to movies and television while griping about the quality and the commercials, go to church but do not care much for sermons, and drink too much in the hope of relaxing—only to find themselves stimulated to even bigger dreams.

Americans love work. It is meat and drink to them. In recent years, they have learned how to play, but they make work of that too. If it is skiing, they throw themselves at it with an effort that would kill a horse. If it is a vacation, they travel at sixty miles an hour, pause only long enough to snap pictures, and then discover what it was they went to see when they get home and look at the photographs.

Americans still like to be handy at all things. College professors go in for making furniture or remodeling an old house in the country. Bankers don aprons and become expert barbecue chefs. Nearly everyone knows how to use tools, make simple repairs to plumbing or electrical fixtures, refinish furniture or paint a wall. Far from being thought a disgrace if he performs these "menial" tasks, a man is thought ridiculous if he does not know how to perform them.

Finish the following exercises.

1. The topic sentence of the text is _____.
2. "They love to think of themselves as tough-minded business men, yet they are <u>push-overs</u> for any hard luck story." Through the context, we can tell the underlined word carries the meaning that Americans are _____ (hard/easy) to overcome or control.
3. American people are very fond of bigness. The statement is _____. (true/false)
4. Americans crowd their highways with cars while <u>complaining about</u> the traffic. The underlined phrase can be replaced by _____ (griping about/gripping about).
5. In recent years, *they have learned how to play, but they make work of that too*. The italicized sentence can be paraphrased as _____.

Text C   What Is Typically American?

Without a doubt, the view upon being typically American differs, from person to person, from country to country. There are many perceptions and many aspects to consider. America is a young country, but it has been a spoiled country for such a long time. As a country which is still establishing its society with more than 300 million people, the U.S. is a bit difficult to describe. "The Salad Bowl" is a popular term describing the many different ingredients that make up American society. But even though the America is a "salad bowl," it certainly has its own characteristics which Americans and foreigners can recognize as distinctly and typically American.

The American society has been built up basically on the same values and ideas. Not only are they on common ground and most people speak the same language, but the country is connected because of communication through media, railroads, highways and a common leader. This gives a feeling of togetherness and belonging. Americans grow up on familiar landmarks and are being influenced in the same way across the country. Each state has its own educational system, but certain values tend to be taught in schools across the nation. It is all about self-esteem and making them feel good about themselves. The U.S. is all about sports and fitness. At the same time many are obese. The number one health risk is in fact obesity. They call it an epidemic, like it is Polio!

It seems as if nobody knows why they are getting fatter. I will blame it on their lifestyle. Someone once said that "Americanism is opposite to tradition." This is because Americanism takes over other countries' traditions. America does not have traditions like other countries. Their lifestyle is a lifestyle of comfort, while people are busy and mobile. All sorts of gadgets, from power-tools to micro-wave ovens, have been created to make life easier. A great example is all of the "drive-in" places you can find. The fast food industry produces cheap super-size food, often with a complimentary biggie fry or jumbo-fry. Many Americans will gladly sit and wait behind ten cars to order food, rather than to go inside. This brings me to another problem. America has become a car-society and is addicted to oil.

There are other things that are typically American. Half the time the ads are of beautiful people running through fields or swimming in the ocean under the sun. This shows the Americans' belief in something better or "The American Dream." If you just work hard enough, you will succeed and get your earned wealth. This shows the work ethic in the U.S. Hard work is valued highly and many Americans are willing to put in long workdays, working overtime for the chance to get ahead. On the other hand, the wages are lower now than they were 40 years ago. There are homeless people everywhere and many people live in suburbs and under poor conditions. What "class" you belong to may be evident from the neighborhood you live in, where you got your education, what kind of car you drive, etc. What counts is common sense and the ability to work one's way up. Sadly, some youngsters tend to drop out of school and end up in tough situations.

Even though the U.S. is all about self-reliance, individualism and self-esteem, religion is very important. A great variety of faiths are represented in the United States. Religion in itself is a value that helps keep people together. State and church are separate and religion is not taught in public schools, but Christian values are often mingled into the concept of American values. Since Americans move so often, their church becomes a network where they can make new friends and be included in the community. This should not be so hard considering that the three qualities that are often emphasized as typically American are informality, a general friendliness to strangers, and a strong community feeling.

Fill in the blanks with proper expressions according to the explanations in the brackets.
1. The view upon being typically American differs, _____ (certainly, definitely), from person to person, from country to country.
2. Not only are they on _____ (a foundation for mutual understanding) and mostly speak the same language, but the country is connected because of communication through media, railroads, highways and a common leader.
3. This is because Americanism _____ (assume right of) other countries traditions, but America does not have traditions like other countries.
4. This brings me to another problem. America has become a car-society and is _____ (to devote oneself habitually to) oil.
5. Sadly some youngsters tend to _____ (quit before graduation) school and end up in tough situations.

Notes

Robert Frost (1874—1963) was an American poet honored frequently during his lifetime, receiving four Pulitzer Prizes. Frost is highly regarded for his realistic depictions of the rural life and his command of American colloquial speech. He wrote many popular and often-quoted poems including "After Apple-Picking," "The Road Not Taken," "Mending Wall," etc.

For Fun

Books to Read
Benjamin Franklin: *Autobiography*
   Benjamin Franklin was not only one of the Founding Fathers of the United States, but also a leading writer, publisher, inventor, diplomat, scientist, and philosopher.

Ralph Waldo Emerson: *Self-Reliance*
   A classic essay on the American value of self-reliance and Emerson's philosophy of moral idealism.

Movies to See
The Pursuit of Happyness
   It is based on a true story of famous self-made millionaire Chris Gardner.

Forrest Gump

Forrest Gump is a simple man with a low I. Q. but good intentions. His mama teaches him the ways of life and leaves him to choose his destiny.

Poem to Read

Can you detect any particular aspect in American character from the following poem? If you will, please underline the lines that impress you the most and explain why.

The Road Not Taken (1915)
By Robert Frost

Two roads diverged in a yellow wood,
And be one traveler, long I stood
And looked down one as far as I could
To where it bent in the undergrowth.

Then took the other, as just as fair,
And having perhaps the better claim,
Because it was grassy and wanted wear;
Though as for that the passing there
Had worn them really about the same.

And both that morning equally lay
In leaves no step had trodden black.
Oh, I kept the first for another day!
Yet knowing how way leads on to way,
I doubted if I should ever come back.

I shall be telling this with a sigh
Somewhere ages and ages hence:
Two roads diverged in a wood, and I—
I took the one less traveled by,
And that has made all the difference.

Unit 3
The American Character (II)

> I'm not English. I'm American. We see all things as possible.
>
> —Norman Mailer

Unit Goals

- To understand basic values and beliefs of American people
- To learn some cultural concepts concerning American character
- To develop critical thinking and intercultural communication skills
- To learn useful words and expressions that describe American character and improve English language skills

Before You Read

1. **Think of some popular American sayings which suggest certain American values or beliefs.**
   For example: Time is money. (Efficiency)
   _____ (   )
   _____ (   )
   _____ (   )
   _____ (   )

2. **Work in groups to find what is inappropriate in each case. Explain why and discuss what you would have done.**
   Situation One
   You were working as a volunteer for the Paralympic Games. One day, you saw an American athlete in a wheelchair that was going up a slope. You came directly to help him move up the slope.

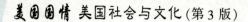

Situation Two

You invited an American friend to your house. The friend went to your house with a gift wrapped up. You thanked the friend and put the gift aside without unwrapping it.

3. How much do you know about Americans?
   Work with your partner. Put a tick(√) in the corresponding column.

Attitudes / Items	Americans like or approve of this	Americans don't like or disapprove of this
wasting time		
allowing social mobility		
doing things the way they've always been done in the past		
being straightforward		
being punctual		
doing things by themselves		
saving money for a rainy day		
taking risks		
judging a worker's worth based on performances		
competing to be the winner or the best		

Start to Read

Text A

1. What are Americans like? What do Americans like? In spite of the great **diversity** in the **ethnic** makeup of America, Americans do share some typical American values, attitudes and beliefs.

2. Watching Americans in action, foreigners sometimes see behavior that seems rude, misguided, or just plain silly. Among them are the following traits, which are characteristically, but certainly not **exclusively**, American.

3. *Hurry, Hurry, Hurry*. Almost every American wears a watch, and, in nearly every room in an American home, there's a clock. "Be on time." "Don't waste time." "Time is money." "Time waits for no one." All these familiar sayings reflect the American **obsession** with **promptness** and efficiency. Students displease their teachers and employees **displease** their bosses when they arrive late. This desire to get the most out  of every minute often makes Americans impatient when they have to wait. The pressure to make every moment count sometimes makes it difficult for Americans to relax.

4. *The Importance of Money*. After visiting the U.S. in the 1830s, the French historian Alexis de Tocqueville wrote, "I know of no country... where the love of money has taken stronger hold..." Americans are often accused of being **materialistic**, of valuing wealth and possession above all else. Money is valued both as a symbol of success and also for a more obvious reason—its purchasing power. Many items which did not even exist 50 years ago are now considered necessities in the American home. In addition, purchases are made in order to "keep up with the Joneses," to show friends that one can afford a bigger house or a fancier car. Also, advertising encourages people to keep buying things far beyond what they need. In the mid-nineteenth century, the American author Henry David Thoreau advised his countrymen: "**Simplify** your needs!" However, Americans have moved in the opposite direction. Now, just as Thoreau predicted, many find that their possessions own them. They must work hard to earn enough money to buy and maintain the many possessions they consider necessities.

5. Yes, Americans love to make a lot of money and spend it on themselves—to buy things that save time, give them pleasure, or serve as status symbols. However, Americans are also very generous and very willing to **donate** money to good causes. The American character includes a strong sense of obligation to help those in need.

6. *Say What You Mean, and Mean What You Say*. Americans believe that

"honesty is the best policy." They are direct and **assertive**. They ask for what they want. In many cultures, respect for those in positions of **authority** keeps people from expressing their true feelings or intentions. In the U.S., however, children often argue with their parents and citizens express opposition to actions of the government. If the soup is cold or the meat is tough, the diner can complain to the waiter. If a teacher is wrong or confusing, a student may say so. If the boss makes a mistake, an employee may politely point it out. Assertive behavior sometimes seems improper and rude to foreigners, but it works well for Americans. In fact, assertiveness is almost a **necessity** in the business world.

7. *The Need to Win*. The **extremely** competitive nature of Americans is often **criticized**. Of course, competition is not always bad. In fact, it **promotes** excellence by encouraging individuals (and businesses) to try to do their best. But the desire to get ahead of others causes people to do things that are unkind and even **dishonest**.

8. *The Practical Outlook*. Americans admire what is practical, fast, efficient, and new. Sometimes they fail to appreciate cultures that prefer more traditional, leisurely ways of doing things. **Conversely**, people from other cultures may dislike the practical, hectic American lifestyle.

9. Despite these traits, which many foreigners may view as faults, Americans are usually considered very likable. Most are friendly, kind-hearted, and eager to help visitors and immigrants. In this nation of immigrants, the foreigner does not remain an outsider for long.

After You Read

Knowledge Focus

1. Answer the following questions.
    1) Why do American people value money so much?
    2) Why do foreigners sometimes think American people are rude and impolite?
    3) What are the advantages and disadvantages of being highly competitive?
    4) How do you understand the statement that "the foreigner does not remain an outsider for long"?

2. Match the examples with the American values the terms illustrate.
    _____ 1) self-reliance   _____ 2) competition
    _____ 3) material wealth   _____ 4) call a spade a spade
    _____ 5) being practical   _____ 6) sense of obligation

a. great emphasis on winning in sports
b. popularity of do-it-yourself policy
c. donating money to churches or schools
d. buying things beyond what they need
e. asking for a raise from the boss
f. action taking priority over words

Language Focus

1. Read the sentences below that contain pairs of opposites in the parentheses. Choose the correct words and write them in the blanks.

   1) Most importantly, if all of us get news and information _____ (inclusively/exclusively) from television, there will be a decline in general literacy.
   2) He is a dutiful son, and he'd do anything rather than _____ (displease/please) his parents.
   3) Our _____ (generous/stingy) hostess heaped our plates with food.
   4) He is an _____ (assertive/indecisive) boy, always insisting on his own rights and opinions.
   5) Nearly all the sports practiced nowadays are _____ (competitive/cooperative), and everybody plays to win.
   6) I feel nothing but contempt for such _____ (dishonest/honest) behavior.
   7) His casual style of dress was _____ (proper/improper) for such a formal dinner.
   8) There are some people who _____ (praise/criticize) the violence in American sports, particularly in football.

2. Use the following expressions to complete the sentences.

make every moment count	point out
keep up with the Joneses	get ahead of
status symbol	keep from
a sense of	ask for

   1) Teachers _____ mistakes so that students will learn the correct way to speak and write English.
   2) If you want to succeed, you have to _____ other competitors.
   3) An expensive car is a(an) _____. It makes the owner seem important.
   4) She bit her lip to _____ crying.
   5) Excuse me. Could I _____ another cup of coffee?
   6) Don't waste time. _____.
   7) You don't have to buy a new house just because your neighbors did. You needn't _____.
   8) _____ humour is a great asset for a person.

3. **Fill in each blank with a suitable preposition.**

   1) Many sayings reflect the American obsession _____ promptness and efficiency.

   2) Advertising encourages people to keep buying things far _____ what they need.

   3) The American character includes a strong sense of obligation to help those _____ need.

   4) In many cultures, respect _____ those in positions of authority keeps people _____ expressing their true feelings or intentions.

   5) In this nation of immigrants, the foreigner does not remain an outsider _____ long.

4. **Proofreading and error correction.**

   The passage contains FIVE errors. Each indicated line contains a maximum of ONE error. In each case, only ONE word is involved.

In short, equality came to mean, in major sense, parity in competition. Its value was as a means to advancement rather than an asset in itself. Like an option in the world of business, it had no intrinsic value but only a value when using. Since the potential value could be realized only by actual movement to a high level, the term "equality" acquired most people exactly the same connotations which the term "upward mobility" has for the social scientist.	1) _____ 2) _____ 3) _____ 4) _____ 5) _____

Comprehensive Work

1. **Identify problems in the following situation: when East meets West, many problems occur.**

Try to put yourself in the shoes of Wang Lin. He invited an American friend Lisa, to his home for a meal. Unfortunately, the occasion gets off to a rather bumpy start.
What has gone wrong? What would you do in such a situation? Analyze the dialogue with your partner.

Wang: Hi! Lisa, welcome! Come in.
Lisa: Thank you for your invitation. It's a lovely room and very warm here.
Wang: My room is very small and untidy. Please sit down and have a cup of tea. You must be tired after the long walk here.
Lisa: What a strange thing to say—your room is perfectly clean and tidy! And as for the walk, I'm very fit, you know. I usually walk for at least half an hour every day. Don't you think walking is a good way to keep fit?

Wang: Yes, I do. Dinner is ready. Please sit at the table.
Lisa: Wow! They look very tasty!
Wang: I'm not a very good cook. Here are only a few cold dishes. Please try this fish, though I'm not very good at cooking fish.
Lisa: This is delicious.

(*Later on in the meal, just before they finish the cold dishes, hot dishes are placed on the table.*)
Lisa: What? There are more?
Wang: Yes. We usually serve eight dishes for our most distinguished guests.
Lisa: If I had known earlier, I would have left some room for the hot dishes. I feel fit to burst at present, and I couldn't eat another mouthful.

2. **Essay Writing.**

Write about the aspects of the American character that impress you most.

Read More

Text B   Go-Go Americans

By Alison R. Lanier

Americans believe no one stands still. If you are not moving ahead, you are falling behind. This attitude results in a nation of people committed to researching, experimenting and exploring. Time is one of the two elements that Americans save carefully, the other being labor.

"We are slaves to nothing but the clock," it has been said. Time is treated as if it were something almost tangible. We budget it, save it, waste it, steal it, kill it, cut it, and account for it; we also charge for it. It is a precious commodity. Many people have a rather acute sense of the shortness of each lifetime. Once the sands have run out of a person's hourglass, they cannot be replaced. We want every minute to count.

A foreigner's first impression of the U.S. is likely to be that everyone is in a rush—often under pressure. City people appear always to be hurrying to get where they are going, restlessly seeking attention in a store, elbowing others as they try to complete their errands. Racing through daytime meals is part of the pace of life in this country. Working time is considered precious.

Others in public eating-places are waiting for you to finish so they too can be served and get back to work within the time allowed. Each person hurries to make room for the next person. If you don't, waiters will hurry you.

You also find drivers will be abrupt and that people will push past you. You will miss smiles, brief conversations, and small courtesies with strangers. Don't take it personally. This is because people value time highly, and they resent someone else "wasting" it beyond a certain courtesy point.

This view of time affects the importance we attach to patience. In the American system of values, patience is not a high priority. Many of us have what might be called "a short fuse." We begin to move restlessly about if we feel time is slipping away without some return—be this in terms of pleasure, work value, or rest. Those coming from lands where time is looked upon differently may find this matter of pace to be one of their most difficult adjustments in both business and daily life.

Many newcomers to the States will miss the opening courtesies of a business call, for example. They will miss the ritual socializing that goes with a welcoming cup of tea or coffee that may be traditional in their own country. They may miss leisurely business chats in a café or coffee house. Normally, Americans do not assess their visitors in such relaxed surroundings over prolonged small talk; much less do they take them out for dinner, or around on the golf course while they develop a sense of trust and rapport. Rapport to most of us is less important than performance. We seek out evidence of past performance rather than evaluate a business colleague through social courtesies. Since we generally assess and probe professionally rather than socially, we start talking business very quickly.

Most Americans live according to time segments laid out in engagement calendars. These calendars may be divided intervals as short as fifteen minutes. We often give a person two or three (or more) segments of our calendar, but in the business world we almost always have other appointments following hard on the heels of whatever we are doing. Time is, therefore, always ticking in our inner ear.

As a result, we work hard at the task of saving time. We produce a steady flow of labor-saving devices; we communicate rapidly through telexes, phone calls or memos rather than through personal contacts, which though pleasant, take longer—especially given our traffic-filled streets. We, therefore, save most personal visiting for after-work hours or for social weekend gatherings.

To us, the impersonality of electronic communication has little or no relation to the importance of the matter at hand. In some countries, no major business is carried out without eye contact, requiring face-to-face conversation. In America, too, a final agreement will normally be signed in person. However, people are meeting increasingly on television screens, conducting "teleconferences" to settle problems not only in this country but also—by satellite—internationally. An increasingly high percentage of normal business is being done these days by voice or electronic device. Mail is slow and uncertain and is growing ever more expensive.

The U. S. is definitely a telephone country. Almost everyone uses the telephone to conduct business, to chat with friends, to make or break engagements, to say their "thank you" to shop and to obtain all kinds of information. Telephones save your feet and endless amounts of time. This is due partly to the fact that the telephone service is good here, whereas the postal service is less efficient. Furthermore, the costs of secretarial labor, printing, and stamps are all soaring. The telephone is quick. We like it. We can do our business and get an answer in a matter of moments. Furthermore, several people can confer together without moving from their desks, even in widely scattered locations. In a big country, that, too, is important.

Some new arrivals will come from cultures where it is considered impolite to work too quickly. Unless a certain amount of time is allowed to elapse, it seems in their eyes as if the task being considered were insignificant, not worthy of proper respect. Assignments are thus felt to be given added weight by the passage of time. In the U. S., however, it is taken as a sign of competence to solve a problem, or fulfill a job successfully, with rapidity. Usually, the more important a task is, the more capital, energy, and attention will be poured into it in order to "get it moving."

Finish the following exercises.
1. What are the two elements that Americans save carefully?
   They are _____ and _____.
2. We budget it, save it, waste it, steal it, kill it, cut it, and account for it; we also charge for it. "It" here refers to _____.
   a. money　　　　　　b. time　　　　　　c. work

3. A foreigner's first impression of the U.S. is likely to be that everyone is _____.
4. Normally Americans do not evaluate a business colleague through social courtesies; they think _____ is more important.
5. In the U.S., assignments are felt to be given added weight by the passage of time. The statement is _____. (true / false)

Text C Time Is Money

What is time? Is it a thing to be saved or spent or wasted, like money? Or is it something we have no control over, like the weather? Is time the same all over the world? That's an easy question, you say. Wherever you go, a minute is 60 seconds, an hour is 60 minutes, a day is 24 hours, and so forth. Well, maybe. But in America, time is more than that. Americans see time as a valuable resource. Maybe that's why they are fond of the expression, "Time is money."

Because Americans believe time is a limited resource, they try to conserve and manage it. People in the U.S. often attend seminars or read books on time management. It seems they all want to organize their time better. Professionals carry around pocket planners—some in electronic form—to keep track of appointments and deadlines. People do all they can to squeeze more life out of their time. The early American hero Benjamin Franklin expressed this view best: "Do you love life? Then do not waste time, for that is the stuff life is made of."

To Americans, punctuality is a way of showing respect for other people's time. Being more than 10 minutes late to an appointment usually calls for an apology, and maybe an explanation. People who are running late often call ahead to let others know of the delay. Of course, the less formal the situation, the less important it is to be exactly on time. At informal get-togethers, for example, people often arrive as much as 30 minutes past the appointed time. But they usually don't try that at work.

American lifestyles show how much people respect the time of others. When people plan an event, they often set the time days or weeks in advance. Once the time is fixed, it takes almost an emergency to change it. If people want to come to your house for a friendly visit, they will usually call first to make sure it is convenient. Only very close friends will just "drop by" unannounced. Also, people hesitate to call others late at night for fear they might be in bed. The time may vary, but most folks think twice about calling after 10:00 p.m.

To outsiders, Americans seem tied to the clock. People in other cultures value relationships more than schedules. In these societies, people don't try to control time, but to experience it. Many Eastern cultures, for example, view time as a cycle. The rhythm of nature—from the passing of the seasons to the monthly cycle of the moon—shapes their view of events. People learn to respond to their environment. As a result, they find it easier to "go with the flow" than Americans, who like plans to be fixed and unchangeable.

Even Americans would admit that no one can master time. Time—like money—slips all too easily through our fingers. And time—like the weather—is very hard to predict. Nevertheless, time is one of life's most precious gifts. And unwrapping it is half the fun.

Finish the following exercises.
1. By saying "Time is money," Americans mean time is very _____.
2. If an American is likely to be late for a formal or business appointment, he or she usually _____.
3. In all situations, Americans try their best to arrive on time. The statement is _____. (true / false)
4. For Americans, the time schedule is flexible and open to changes. The statement is _____. (true / false)
5. In the U.S., if people want to come to your house for a friendly visit, they will usually _____. It is only very close friends who can _____.
6. In the U.S., people can call each other any time they want. The statement is _____. (true / false)
7. Many Eastern cultures view time as a cycle, and thus they value time _____ (more / less) importantly than American people do.

Notes

1. **Norman Kingsley Mailer** (1923—2007) was an American novelist, journalist, essayist, poet, playwright, screenwriter, and film director. Mailer is considered an innovator of narrative nonfiction, a genre sometimes called New Journalism.
2. **Alexis de Tocqueville** (1805—1859) was a French political thinker and historian best known for his *Democracy in America* and *The Old Regime and*

the Revolution. In both of these works, he explored the effects of the rising equality of social conditions on the individual and the state in Western societies.

3. **Henry David Thoreau** (1817—1862) was an American author, naturalist, transcendentalist, tax resister, development critic, sage writer and philosopher. He is best known for his book *Walden*, a reflection upon simple living in natural surroundings, and his essay, "Civil Disobedience," an argument for individual resistance to civil government in moral opposition to an unjust state.

Books to Read

David Potter: *People of Plenty: Economic Abundance and American Character*
    American people's distinctive character has been shaped by economic abundance.

Spencer Johnson: *Who Move My Cheese: An Amazing Way to Deal with Change in Your Work and in Your Life*
    A best-seller about how to cope with a changing work place.

Jack London: *Martin Eden*
    A novel about a hard-working young man walking all his way up to fulfill his dream as a writer and only to find that every dream has a price.

Movies to See

The Great Gatsby
    A writer and Wall Street trader, Nick, finds himself drawn to the past and lifestyle of his millionaire neighbor, Jay Gatsby.

October Sky
    The true story of Homer Hickam, a coal miner's son who, against his father's wishes, was inspired by the first Sputnik launch to build rockets.

Unit 4
Religion in the U.S.

> The care of every man's soul belongs to himself.
> —Thomas Jefferson

Unit Goals

- To get a general knowledge of religion in America
- To learn the role religion plays in American life
- To get acquainted with some religious terms on American religions
- To develop critical thinking and intercultural communication skills
- To learn useful words and expressions concerning religion in the U.S. and improve English language skills

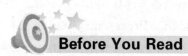

Consider the following questions.

1. What might be the reasons that make people go for certain religious beliefs? What can religious beliefs bring to people's life?
2. What is your belief, if you have any?
3. Read the quotation by Thomas Jefferson. What do you think he meant? How could this belief affect religion in the United States?

Start to Read

Text A   Religion in the United States

1. The **fundamental** American belief in individual freedom and the right of individuals to practice their own religion is at the center of religious experience in the United States. The great **diversity** of ethnic backgrounds has produced religious **pluralism**; most of the religions of the world are now practiced in the United States. 90 percent of Americans say that they believe in God, although not all of them **participate** in traditional religious organizations. About 80 percent of Americans are **Christians**, about 2 percent are Jewish, and another 4 percent belong to other religious faiths such as Islam, Buddhism, and Hinduism.*

2. Religion has always played an important role in the history of the United States. The **Catholic** faith was first brought to the North American continent by the Spanish in the 1500s. For the next 300 years, Catholic missionaries and settlers from Spain and then Latin America came to what is now California and the Southwest. In the 1600s, the European settlers began establishing colonies along the east coast of North America. Although there were some Catholics, the vast majority of the European settlers were **Protestants**, most from England. As the new nation formed, it was the Protestant branch of the Christian faith that had the strongest effect on the development of the religious climate in the United States.

The Development of Protestantism

3. The Protestant branch of the Christian faith broke away from the Roman Catholic Church in Europe in the sixteenth century because of important differences in religious beliefs. (The Eastern Orthodox branch of the Christian faith had separated from the Roman Catholic Church in 1054.) At the time of Protestant Reformation, the Roman Catholic Church was the center of religious life in Western European countries; the Catholic pope and the priests played the role of parent to the people in **spiritual** matters. They told people what was right

and wrong, and they granted them **forgiveness** for sins against God and the Catholic faith.

4. The Protestants, on the other hand, insisted that all individuals must stand alone before God. If people sinned, they should seek their forgiveness directly from God rather than from a priest speaking in God's name. In place of the power and authority of priests, Protestants **substituted** what they called the "priesthood of all believers." This meant that every individual was solely responsible for his or her own relationship with God.

5. After the Protestants broke away from the Catholic Church, they found that they could not agree among themselves about many beliefs. Therefore, the Protestants began to form separate churches, called **denominations**. There was much bitterness among some of the religious beliefs in the 1600s, and many Protestant denominations experienced religious **persecution**. A number of people were even killed because of their beliefs. The result of this persecution was that many Protestants were ready to leave their native countries in order to have freedom to practice their particular religious beliefs. **Consequently**, among the early settlers who came to America in the 1600s, there were many Protestants seeking religious freedom.

6. The lack of any established national religion in America **appealed** strongly to European Protestants, whether or not they were being persecuted. A large number of Protestant denominations were established in America. At first, some denominations hoped to force their views and beliefs on others, but the colonies were simply too large for any one denomination to gain control over the others. The idea of separation of church and state became accepted. When the Constitution was **adopted** in 1789, the government was forbidden to establish a national church; no denomination was to be favored over the others. The government and the church had to remain separate. Under these conditions, a great **variety** of different Protestant denominations developed and grew, with each denomination having a "live and let live" attitude toward the others. Diversity was accepted and strengthened. Today, the various Protestant denominations have completely separate church organizations, and although there were many similarities, there are also significant differences in their religious teachings and beliefs.

The Protestant Heritage: Self-Improvement

7. Protestantism has been a powerful force in shaping the values and beliefs of Americans. One of the most important values associated with American

Protestantism is the value of self-improvement. **Christianity** often emphasizes the natural sinfulness of human nature. Unlike Catholics, Protestants do not go to priests for forgiveness of their sins; individuals are left alone before God to improve themselves and ask for God's **guidance**, forgiveness, and grace. For this reason, Protestantism has traditionally encouraged a strong and restless desire for self-improvement.

8. The need for self-improvement, once established, reaches far beyond self-improvement in the purely moral or religious sense. It can be seen in countless books, which explain how people can be happier and more successful in life by improving everything from their vocabulary to their tennis game, or even their whole personality. Books of this type are often referred to as "self-help" books, and many are best-sellers. They are natural products of a culture in which people believe that "God helps those who help themselves." In addition, Americans attend thousands of self-help seminars and support group meetings to help them stop smoking or drinking, lose weight, be better parents, have happier relationships, and develop self-confidence.

Material Success, Hard Work, and Self-Discipline

9. The achievement of material success is probably the most widely respected form of self-improvement in the United States. The **philosophy**—commonly called the Protestant work **ethic**—stresses the moral value of work, self-discipline, and personal responsibility. According to this ethic, people prove their worth to themselves and to God by working hard, being honest and thrifty, and avoiding luxury, **excessive** pleasure, and waste. The **accumulation** of wealth is not considered evil unless it leads to a life of idleness and sin. The Protestant work ethic has much in common with the American emphasis on financial success, practicality, efficiency and self-sufficiency.

10. Protestant leaders view the work of all people as holy, not just that of priests. They also believe that the **capacity** for self-discipline was a holy characteristic blessed by God. Self-discipline is often defined as the willingness to save and invest one's money rather than spend it on immediate pleasures. Protestant tradition, therefore, may have played an important part in creating a good **climate** for the industrial growth of the United States.

Volunteerism and Humanitarianism

11. The idea of self-improvement includes more than achieving material gain through hard work and self-discipline. It also includes the idea of improving oneself by helping others. Individuals, in other words, make themselves into better persons by contributing some of their time or money to **charitable**, educational, or religious causes that are designed to help others. This philosophy is sometimes called **volunteerism** or **humanitarianism**.

12. Historically, some of the extremely wealthy-Americans have made **generous** contributions to help others. In the early 1900s, for example, Andrew Carnegie, a famous American businessman, gave away more than $300 million to help support schools and universities and to build public libraries in thousands of communities in the United States. The motive for humanitarianism and volunteerism is strong: many Americans believe that they should devote part of their time and wealth to religious or humanitarian causes in order to be acceptable in the eyes of God and in the eyes of other Americans. Many businesses encourage their employees to do volunteer work, and individuals may get tax deductions for money given to charity.

* Source of data：埃塞尔·蒂尔斯基、马丁·蒂尔斯基编著. (2006) 美国制度与文化(引进版)[M]. 北京：中国人民大学出版社。

After You Read

Knowledge Focus

1. Answer the following questions.
   1) Why did Protestants break away from the Catholic Church?
   2) Why did many Protestants leave their native land to settle in America?
   3) What is the essence of "Protestant work ethic"? What has the ethic brought to the United States?
   4) Why did the American Constitution adopt the policy of "separation of church and state"? What is the purpose?
   5) What is humanitarianism? Is this philosophy part of your belief?
2. Mark each statement with T if it is true or F if it is false.
   1) Protestants and Christians are all Catholic. _____
   2) The official national religion of the United States is Protestantism. _____
   3) No single church has become the center of religious life in the United States because the emphasis is on the individual, not a particular church. _____
   4) Most of the settlers who came to colonial America to escape religious persecution in

Europe were Catholics. _____

5) Protestant belief requires the strict obeying of rigid rules in organized religious practice. _____

6) "Priesthood of all believers" means every priest should be responsible for the believers. _____

7) The policy of "separation of church and state" protects religious freedom. _____

8) The protestant branch broke away from the Roman Catholic Church because the Protestants and Catholics have different faiths. _____

Language Focus

1. Match the words and definitions.

   ____ 1) sin   a. people who meet to encourage each other
   ____ 2) denomination   b. the religious leader of Roman Catholic church
   ____ 3) persecution   c. an order that forbids something
   ____ 4) humanitarianism   d. a particular religious body
   ____ 5) ban   e. cruelty; causing suffering
   ____ 6) eternal   f. giving time to serve others without pay
   ____ 7) support group   g. improving life for others
   ____ 8) volunteerism   h. continuing forever
   ____ 9) solely   i. a morally wrong act
   ____ 10) Pope   j. only

2. Use the following expressions to complete the sentences.

break away from	give away
force...on	has much / little in common
create a good climate for	ask for

   1) We two _____ so _____ that we could get along very well with each other.
   2) The little boy finally _____ the stranger and raced for the door.
   3) Don't _____ your views and ideas _____ others.
   4) The local government has _____ the economic development and overseas investment.
   5) He decided to _____ everything he possessed and to become a monk.
   6) A Mr. Simpson from Sydney is _____ the manager.

3. Fill in each blank with a suitable preposition.

   1) 90 percent of Americans say that they believe in God, although not all of them participate _____ traditional religious organizations.
   2) It was the Protestant branch of the Christian faith that had the strongest effect _____ the development of the religious climate in the United States.

3) They told people what was right and wrong, and they granted them forgiveness for sins _____ God and the Catholic faith.
4) If people sinned, they should seek their forgiveness directly from God rather than from a priest speaking _____ God's name according to Protestantism.
5) The colonies were simply too large for any one denomination to gain control _____ the others.
6) Protestantism has traditionally encouraged a strong and restless desire _____ self-improvement.
7) The capacity _____ self-discipline was a holy characteristic blessed by God.
8) Self-discipline is often defined as the willingness to save and invest one's money rather than spend it _____ immediate pleasures.

4. Proofreading and error correction.
   The passage contains FIVE errors. Each indicated line contains a maximum of ONE error. In each case, only ONE word is involved.

| Americans have long committed to the ideal of religious diversity. Instead of a shared religion, the United States is greatly influenced by some observers have called "civil religion"—a widespread acceptance of a unifying set of values that bind Americans with a shared code of behavior. While try to maintain a posture of separation between church and state, Americans have attempted to balance that posture by using amorphous religious rhetoric to legitimize certain standards of ethics and behavior. | 1) _____
 2) _____

 3) _____
 4) _____

 5) _____ |

Comprehensive Work

1. Share ideas with your partners.
   Times of crisis often bring out the best in people. When a house burns down and a family is homeless, or when there is a natural disaster such as a flood or earthquake, people often volunteer to help. Work in groups of four, think of an event that you have  experienced, or one that you have heard about, talk with your partners of what happened and how people helped.

2. **Use the Internet and write a report.**

The following people are highly regarded for their humanitarian work. Choose one and find out why the person is or was important. Search for the right information on the Internet and then write a report about your findings.

Martin Luther King, Jr. *Mother Teresa*
Oskar Schindler *Jimmy Carter*

Read More

Text B   Puritanism

By Francis J. Bremer

The relationship between religious faith and political culture has long been a staple of public discourse. "Puritans" and "Puritanism" are terms likely to be invoked in such discussions, despite being references to centuries-old religious subjects. Nevertheless, puritanism is one of the least understood parts of America's—and Britain's—heritage. The word "puritan" is likely to be associated with "prudish," "sexually repressed," "prohibitionist," "busybody snoops"—the types of things that led the twentieth-century social critic H. L. Mencken to define puritanism as "the fear that someone, somewhere, may be happy." The image of puritans as theocrats, regicides, witch-burners, Indian killers, and bigoted heresy hunters has long been entrenched in popular culture. Most of these are distortions if not absolute falsehoods, but the stereotypes are deeply embedded.

Among the most fundamental yet disputed aspects of the subject is the definition of puritanism. Whereas other religious movements of the sixteenth and seventeenth centuries—Lutheranism, Catholicism, Genevan Calvinism, among others—became institutionalized so that there were official statements of faith and formal membership in churches, puritanism never achieved that type of clear identity. It was a movement defined in part by the self-identification of men and women who referred to themselves as "godly" or "professors" and partly by their enemies, who scorned them as "precisians," and "hypocrites." The actual label "puritan" was originally a term of opprobrium used by their enemies, though eventually adopted by the members of the movement. Some scholars have come to look at puritanism as a temperament and to talk of the "puritan character." Recent research points to the varieties of puritanism, pointing out that the experience, beliefs, and behavior of these believers were often uniquely shaped by particular circumstances they faced.

At the simplest level, puritans were those who sought to reform themselves and their society by purifying their churches of the remnants of Roman Catholic teachings and practice then found in post-Reformation England during the mid-sixteenth century, such as using clerical vestments and kneeling to receive the Lord's Supper. They were particularly insistent that individual believers had access to the Scriptures, the Word of God, in their own language. They agitated for the placement of university-trained preachers in every parish. They believed that England as a political nation must be committed to opposing the forces of Rome throughout Christendom. While Englishmen who were not labeled puritans might support some or all of these objectives, those who bore the label were seen as most committed and most fervent in advancing them.

At the heart of puritanism was the attempt to transform society by first using grace to make God's will one's own. By doing so the individual would lead an exemplary life that would persuade others—family, friends, and the broader community—to follow the path of right belief and behavior. When puritans achieved political power—in America in the colonies they established and in England following the Civil Wars of the 1640s—they were able to employ instruments of power as well as those of persuasion. The responsibilities that came with power brought new challenges but did not alter the puritan objective to make society a godly kingdom. Their understanding of God's will led them to promote education, to redefine marriage and other institutions, and to adopt participatory forms of government. While puritans as a specific group are no longer with us, the impact of those initiatives on America and England continues to be felt.

Finish the following exercises.
1. Puritanism is exclusively an American heritage. The statement is _____.
   (true / false)
2. Which of the following images are NOT likely to be associated with the Puritans? _____.
   a. Prohibitionists   b. Theocrats   c. Precisians   d. Hedonists

3. Fill in the blanks: At the simplest level, puritans were those who _____ by purifying their churches of the remnants of Roman Catholic teachings and practice. At the heart of puritanism was the attempt to transform society by first using grace to _____.

Text C Community Hero: Millard and Linda Fuller

The American recipe for success and happiness for a young couple is one educated, beautifully turned-out wife, combined with one super-successful businessman husband, two beautiful children and a great, big, beautifully decorated house. This is the American Dream. Millard and Linda Fuller, co-founders of Habitat for Humanity, the non-profit organization that has built over 65,000 houses for people who need them, had the two kids, the well-educated wife and the super-successful businessman husband. They even had the architect's plans to build their beautiful dream house. There was only one problem: the Fullers were miserable in their marriage. When a marriage is in trouble, some couples start having affairs, others get a divorce, and some couples start building a bigger house. For Millard and Linda Fuller, the answer was not building a bigger house; it was building houses for others.

The Fullers are acclaimed for starting and running Habitat for Humanity, which now has over 2,000 chapters worldwide, and brings Christians, Jews, men and women, corporate people and blue-collar folk together to provide homes for families in need. While they have received recognition for their accomplishments through this organization, they are also truly heroic for the things they gave up, for their ability to throw out a recipe that was sour for them.

Recalls Linda Fuller, "After so many years of marriage, we had two kids and I had finished my college degree. I was really lonely because Millard was working every night. We had all the money and clothes we wanted, and were talking to an architect about building a huge house."

"After I finished my classes and had time to think, I realized I was lonely and miserable. I went to New York and stayed there for a few weeks."Millard remembers about that time, "I wanted to make money, buy big cars, have a big house. My business was first. Everything else was second, my wife and our kids. I worked all day, came home, had supper, and went back to work. My marriage suffered, our relationship suffered, while my business grew."

"By the time Millard came to New York, it was like death walked in the door. He realized we were in crisis. I knew I wanted our marriage to work, but I didn't see how that could happen with him working all the time," says Linda.

Discouraged and confused, but still talking, the two went to see a movie ironically called *Never Too Late*. Too distraught to sit through the movie, Linda and Millard walked the streets of New York and wound up sitting on the steps of a building. "We shared with each other how our marriage had gone wrong and we both wanted to make it right. The next morning we hailed a taxi and the driver said, 'Congratulations, you're riding in a brand new taxi no one has ridden in.' We felt it was a sign that we were on a brand-new adventure."

The Fullers sold everything they had and gave every dime away in their search for peace. However, the Fullers weren't content to simply give money away to a cause. Recalls Millard, "We wanted to make our lives count."

At first, Millard began working at a small African-American college, using his business sense to get money for the struggling school. Then, the Fullers went to live in a small community called Koinonia Farm, located near Americus, Georgia. While living in this community, the Fullers, along with other members of Koinonia Farm, began developing an idea for building low-income housing.

"It was so wonderful to be on the same road," Linda recalls. "After we lived in the Koinonia Farm, we wanted to try building homes in developing countries. We moved to Africa for three years and I had a home delivery there." Returning to Georgia, the Fullers lived in a poor community and observed their surroundings.

Habitat for Humanity was formally created in 1976. The Fullers' philosophy is simple: every person on this planet should have a simple and decent place to live. While volunteers from the community and from outside provide free labor and materials, the family who receives the house must put in

300 hours of work themselves. Their hard work is considered the down payment.

Habitat for Humanity is a presence all over the world. Their international headquarter is in Americus, Georgia. The Fullers see Americus as their base of operations to help organize and support the many national and international chapters. Homes have been built in 79 countries, and in all of the 50 states of the U.S.

Today, the Fuller children are in the Habitat business, where friends and associates like Jimmy Carter work with them. Starting and growing Habitat is an achievement in and of itself, but figuring out how to save a marriage and create something so beautiful together is why I consider the Fullers to be my heroes.

Answer the following question.
Why are the Fullers considered as heroes? What is Habitat for Humanity?

Proper Names

Georgia   n.   佐治亚州(在美国南部,首府为亚特兰大 Atlanta)

Notes

1. **Thomas Jefferson** (1743—1826) was the third President of the United States (1801—1809), the principal author of the *Declaration of Independence* (1776), and one of the most influential Founding Fathers for his promotion of the ideals of republicanism in the United States.
2. **Andrew Carnegie** (1835—1919), known as the King of Steel, built the steel industry in the United States, and in the process, became one of the wealthiest men in America. Carnegie believed that individuals should progress through hard work, but he also felt strongly that the wealthy should use their fortunes for the benefit of society. "He who dies rich, dies disgraced," he often said. Few Americans have been left untouched by Andrew Carnegie's generosity. His contributions of more than five million dollars established 2,500 libraries in small communities throughout the country.

3. **Jimmy Carter** (1924—   ) was the thirty-ninth President of the United States, serving

from 1977 to 1981, and the recipient of the 2002 Nobel Peace Prize. After leaving office, Carter and his wife founded the Carter center. He has traveled extensively to conduct peace negotiations and establish relief efforts; he is also a key figure in the Habitat for Humanity project.

For Fun

Books to Read

Max Weber: *The Protestant Ethic and the Spirit of Capitalism*

Weber suggested that the psychological effects of predestinarian theology fostered an ethic that fueled economic growth in England and America.

Nathaniel Hawthorne: *The Scarlet Letter*

Set in early colonial times in New England, this classic story reveals the impact of an act of passion in a Puritan society.

Herman Melville: *Billy Budd*

A classic American story of an innocent young man on a ship who is accused of treason by another sailor who dislikes him.

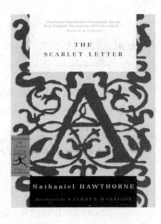

Movies to See

Saved

A comedy about teenagers in a religious school who have difficulty deciding what is really the right thing to do.

A Simple Plan

Two brothers find a bag of stolen money and must decide what to do with it.

Unit 5

The Mythical American West

> This ever-retreating frontier of free land is the key to American development.
>
> —Thomas Jefferson

Unit Goals

- To get a general knowledge of American frontier life
- To get to know some American values developed from American frontier experience
- To learn the role American frontier plays in shaping traditional American values
- To develop critical thinking and intercultural communication skills
- To learn useful words and expressions concerning American frontier life and improve English language skills

Before You Read

1. **Consider the following questions.**
   1) What is a frontier?
   2) How much do you know about American frontier life?
   3) Name some of the movies you have seen about the Old West. Talk about them.

2. **Preview vocabulary.**
   Work with a partner to answer the questions. Make sure you understand the meaning of the words in italics.
   1) If "spiritual" has to do with your soul, and "mental" has to do with your mind, what does *physical* has to do with?
   2) If people are discussing a *controversial* topic, such as religion or politics, would you expect there to be a lot of agreement or disagreement?

3) If we say that the settlement of the western frontier had an *impact* on American culture, do we mean that it had some influence or that it was not very important?
4) If you wanted to *reinforce* your cowboy image, what would you wear?
5) Would someone who had a "can-do" attitude be an optimist or a *pessimist*?

Start to Read

Text A The Impact of the American Frontier

1. Although the American **civilization** took over and replaced the **frontier** more than a century ago, the **heritage** of the frontier is still evident in the United States today. Many people are still **fascinated** by the frontier because it has been particularly important in shaping American values. When Ronald Reagan was president in the 1980s, he liked to recall the image of life on the frontier. He was often photographed on his western ranch—chopping wood or riding his horse, and wearing his cowboy hat. President George W. Bush **reinforced** this cowboy image by inviting members of the press to photograph him on his Texas ranch, wearing his cowboy boots and hat.

The Frontier Experience

2. The frontier experience began when the first colonists settled on the east coast of the continent in the 1600s. It ended in about 1890 when the last western lands were settled. The American frontier **consisted** of the relatively unsettled regions of the United States, usually found in the western part of the country. Here, both land and life were more rugged and **primitive** than in the more settled eastern part. As one frontier area was settled, people began moving farther west into the next unsettled area, sweeping aside the Native Americans as they went. By settling one frontier area after another, Americans moved across an entire continent that was 2,700 miles wide. They came to believe that it was their destiny to control all the land, and **eventually** they did. The Native Americans were given small portions of land, called **reservations**,

to control, but the United States government broke many promises and created much misery for the Indian nations.

3. While more Americans have a more balanced view of the settling of the West, many Americans still see aspects of the frontier, its people, and their beliefs as **inspiring** examples of traditional American values in their original and purest form. How did the frontier movement, which lasted more than two centuries, help to shape these basic American values?

4. To be sure, the frontier provided many inspiring examples of hard work as forests were turned into towns, and towns into large cities. The competitive race for success was rarely more colorful or **adventurous** than on the western **frontier**. The rush for gold in California, for silver in Montana, and for fertile land in all the western territories provided endless stories of high adventure. When it was announced that almost 2 million acres of good land in Oklahoma would be opened for settlement in April 1889, thousands of settlers gathered on the border waiting for the exact time to be announced. When it was, they **literally** raced into the territory in wagons and on horseback to claim the best land they could find for themselves.

The starting line for the first Oklahoma Land Rush, April 22, 1889

5. Although daily life on the frontier was usually less **dramatic** than the frontier adventure stories would lead one to believe, even the ordinary daily life of frontier men and women **exemplified** national values in a form which seemed purer to many Americans than the life of those living in the more settled, more **cultivated** eastern United States.

The Frontier Heritage of America

6. Individualism, **self-reliance**, and equality of opportunity have perhaps been the values most closely associated with the frontier heritage of America. Throughout their history, Americans have tended to view the frontier settler as the model of the free individual. This is probably because there was less control over the individual on the frontier than anywhere else in the United States. There were few laws and few established social or political institutions to **confine** people living on the frontier. In the United States, where freedom from outside social controls has traditionally been valued, the frontier has been **idealized**, and it still serves as a basis for a **nostalgic** view of early United States, a simpler time that was lost when the country became **urbanized** and more complex. Many people living in the West today still hold these beliefs about freedom from government controls.

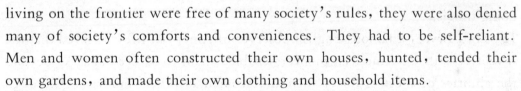

Self-Reliance and the Rugged Individualists

7. Closely associated with the frontier ideal of the free individual is the ideal of self-reliance. If the people living on the frontier were free of many society's rules, they were also denied many of society's comforts and conveniences. They had to be self-reliant. Men and women often constructed their own houses, hunted, tended their own gardens, and made their own clothing and household items.

8. The self-reliant frontiersman has been idealized by Americans who have made him the model of the classic American male hero with **rugged** individualism. This hero is a man who has been made physically tough and rugged by the conditions of frontier life. He is skilled with guns and other weapons. He needs no help from others. Often, he appears in stories as alone, unmarried and without children. Standing alone, he can meet all the dangers which life on the frontier brings. He is strong enough to **extend** his protection beyond himself to others.

9. There are two types of heroic rugged individualists. Each is drawn from a different stage of life on the frontier. In the early frontier, which existed before the Civil War of the 1860s, the main struggle was man against the **wilderness**. Daniel Boone is probably the best-known hero of this era. The second type of heroic rugged individualist is drawn from the last phase of the western frontier, which lasted from the 1860s until the 1890s. By this time, the wilderness was largely **conquered**. The struggle now was no longer man against nature, but man against man. Cattlemen and cowboys fought against farmers, **outlaws**, Native Americans, and each other for control of the remaining western lands. The traditions of law and order were not yet well established, and physical violence was frequent. The frontier became known as "the Wild West."

10. It is not surprising, then, that the hero drawn from this period is primarily a fighter. He is admired for his ability to beat other men in fistfights, or to win in a gunfight. The principle source of his heroism is his physical **prowess** and he is strong enough to defeat two or three ordinary men at one time. This rugged individualist is typically a defender of good against evil.

Inventiveness and the Can-Do Spirit

11. While the frontier idealized the rugged individual as the great American hero, it also respected the inventive individual. The need for self-reliance on the frontier encouraged a spirit of inventiveness. Frontier men and women not only had to provide most of their daily life essentials, but they were also constantly facing new problems and situations which demanded new solutions. Under these circumstances, they soon learned to experiment with new ways of doing things.

12. Lord Bryce, a famous English observer of American life, believed that the inventive skills of American pioneers enabled them to succeed at tasks beyond the abilities of most ordinary men and women in other countries. Although Americans in the more settled eastern regions of the United States created many of the most important inventions in the new nation, the western frontier had the effect of spreading the spirit of inventiveness throughout the population and helping it to become a national character **trait**.

13. The willingness to experiment and invent led to another American trait, a "can-do" spirit, or a sense of **optimism** that every problem has a solution. Americans like to believe that a difficult problem can be solved immediately—an impossible one may take a little longer. They take pride in meeting **challenges** and overcoming difficult **obstacles**. This can-do spirit has traditionally given Americans a sense of optimism about themselves and their country. Many like to say that if the United States can land a man on the moon, no problem on earth is impossible.

Equality of Opportunity

14. The frontier is an expression of individual freedom and self-reliance in its purest forms, and it is also a pure expression of the ideal of equality of opportunity. On the western frontier, there was more of a tendency for people to treat each other as social equals than there was in the more settled eastern regions of the country. On the frontier, the highest importance was placed on what people could do in their own lifetime. Hardly any notice was taken of their ancestors. Frontier people were fond of saying, "What's above the ground is more important than what's beneath the ground."

15. Because so little attention was paid to a person's family background, the frontier offered a new beginning for many Americans who were seeking opportunities to advance themselves. One English visitor to the United States in the early 1800s **observed** that if Americans experienced disappointment or failure in business, in politics, or even in love, they moved west to make a new beginning. The frontier offered millions of Americans a source of hope for a fresh start in the competitive race for success and for a better life.

16. The frontier provided the space and conditions which helped to **strengthen** the American ideals of individual freedom, self-reliance, and equality of opportunity. On the frontier, these ideals were **enlarged** and made workable. Frontier ideas and customs were continuously passed along to the more settled parts of the United States as newer frontier regions took the place of older ones during a westward march of settlers which lasted more than two centuries. In this way, many of the frontier values became national values.

After You Read

Knowledge Focus

1. Answer the following questions.
    1) What are the three values that are traditionally associated with the frontier heritage?
    2) What two new values are introduced in this text?
    3) What are the two types of rugged individualists?
    4) How do you understand the saying "What's above the ground is more important than what's beneath the ground"?

2. Mark each statement true (T) or false (F).
    1) The frontier experience began in about 1890 and is still continuing in the American West today. _____
    2) One reason why many Americans people are still fascinated by the frontier period is that it represents a time when the traditional basic American values were expressed in their purest form. _____

3) The settling of the frontier did little to affect the lives of the American Indians. _____
4) The can-do spirit came from the willingness of the pioneers to work together on a cooperative project for the good of all. _____
5) On the frontier, family name and ancestry were more important than what a person could do. _____
6) The American frontiersman is the model of the classic American male hero, who always appeared together with his fellow brothers. _____
7) There are two types of heroic rugged individualists: man against wilderness and man against man. _____
8) During the frontier period, people usually paid a lot of attention to a person's family background and ancestry. _____

Language Focus

1. **Use context clues to choose the correct words to fill in the blanks.**

| fascinated | nostalgic | exemplified |
| obstacle | literally | evident |

1) Americans like to remember the days on the frontier; they feel _____ about the Old West.
2) In order to succeed, people living on the frontier had to overcome many _____.
3) Little John was so naughty that he _____ became a pain in the neck to the whole family.
4) His age was _____ in his wrinkled hands.
5) If you are reading a book that is so interesting and you can't put it down, you are _____ by the book.
6) Frontier people were good examples of the American national values; these people _____ American individualism and optimism.

2. **Find out word partners.**

Match the word partners to form collocations, and then use the correct collocations in the paragraph.

_____ 1) unsettled   a. fathers
_____ 2) law-abiding   b. spirit
_____ 3) can-do   c. individualism
_____ 4) founding   d. citizens
_____ 5) physical   e. region
_____ 6) rugged   f. prowess

Many Americans believe that when the _____ wrote the Constitution, they meant to ensure the right of the people to own guns. They would argue that

_____ should be allowed to keep guns in their homes. The frontier strengthened the tradition of owning guns because it was a (an) _____ and settlers needed guns for hunting and protection. They had to be tough, and part of the frontier legacy is the _____ and _____ of Western movie heroes. Frontier settlers were also known for their inventiveness and their _____.

3. **Fill in the blanks with the proper forms of the words in the brackets.**
   1) They tried to _____ (civilization) the tribe, but I thought it would be better for the people to remain as they were.
   2) You had better _____ (reservation) the money for future need.
   3) His friend's words _____ (inspiring) him to try again.
   4) Mr. Robinson is very fond of _____ (adventurous), and his wish was to travel around the world.
   5) Do you place much _____ (reliant) on your doctor?
   6) The weather is _____ (idealize) for an outing.
   7) We want to _____ (strength) our ties with them.
   8) I'd like to have this photograph _____ (large), please.

4. **Proofreading and error correction.**

   The passage contains FIVE errors. Each indicated line contains a maximum of ONE error. In each case, only ONE word is involved.

A large part of what make the West cohere is its history. For most Americans the West is defined primary by its frontier heritage. The West is the land of explorers and fur trading "mountain men," gold rushes and Indian conflicts, cowboys, overland trails and hard pioneers. This "West of the imagination" became the focal point for a immense popular-culture industry was incessantly portrayed in art and music, a vast literature and above all in movies and on television.	1) _____ 2) _____ 3) _____ 4) _____ 5) _____

Comprehensive Work

1. **Share ideas with your team members.**

   Americans believe in the importance of teaching their children to be self-reliant. Perhaps this philosophy has something to do with how the frontier was settled. Ellen Goodman, a popular columnist, observes:

   The whole country was settled by one generation of leavers after the next—people who moved to a new frontier or a new neighborhood or a new job, who continually left relationships for opportunities. It was considered unreasonable, almost unpatriotic, for parents to "cling." And it still is.

The result of this is an emphasis on raising children to live independently and separate from their parents. The goal of parenting in America is to make children competent and confident enough to "leave the nest." What do you think of this philosophy? Compare and contrast this philosophy of raising children with the child-raising philosophy in China. What has caused the differences?

In America	In China
Children voluntarily move out of the family before marriage.	
Children are expected to repay the money loaned by their parents for their university education.	
Parents emphasize fostering independence from an early age.	
Children are most likely to be expected to work while they are studying.	

2. Essay Writing.

The American people attach great importance to individualism. What do you think are the factors that have helped Americans form such a belief? Should Chinese people welcome individualism?

Read More

Text B   Rugged Individuals

I would rather sit on a pumpkin, and have it all to myself, than to be crowded on a velvet cushion.

—Henry David Thoreau

Since the early days of European settlement, America has been seen as the place where enterprising individuals, freed from the restrictions and class structure of the Old World, could go as far as their abilities and capacity for hard work would take them. The accent is on the individual.

Reverence for the individual runs deep in the American character. In the late nineteenth century, this philosophy of individualism took shape in a type of national hero that became known as "the rugged individual." The rugged individual is the man who succeeds through his own efforts, separating himself from the crowd by virtue of his self-reliance, self-discipline, nerves of steel, hard work, native shrewdness, "can-do" spirit, and, up to his image, his enduring popularity in the public imagination reflects the esteem in which Americans hold "the self-made man," the man who "does it his way," the "true competitor."

In unrestrained competition, victory goes to the strong, the ambitious, the ingenious, the industrious, the "fittest to survive," and their rewards as victors are proportioned to the contributions of their labors to the total product, as justice requires; they get what they deserve, in short. In the strife among competing individuals, the production of wealth is increased while its distribution runs according to merits. Poverty is due to the indolence, lack of initiative, improvidence, dearth of ambition or the restlessness of the poor themselves.

This world-view of human beings was reinforced by the rise and spread of Darwinism—the world-view of biological determinism for the activities of all living things. According to that theory the evolution of all life had been and is through the struggle for existence, natural selection, and the survival of the fittest, the victors, in that competition. The idea of civilization was limited to humanity, but individualism assimilated mankind to the whole order of living things under one iron law.

Answer the following questions.
1. What are the major characteristics of the "Rugged Individuals"?
2. What are the key ideas of Darwinism or the theory of evolution?
3. What may be the author's attitude towards those living in poverty?

Proper Names

Texas	n.	得克萨斯(美国州名)
California	n.	加利福尼亚(美国州名)
Montana	n.	蒙大拿(美国州名)
Oklahoma	n.	俄克拉荷马(美国州名)

Notes

1. **Ronald Reagan** (1911—2004) was the 40th President of the United States. During his term, Reagan ordered a massive military buildup in an arms race with the Soviet Union, forgoing the previous strategy of détente.
2. **Daniel Boone** (1734—1820) was an American pioneer and hunter whose frontier exploits made him one of the first folk heroes of the United States. Boone is most famous for his exploration and settlement of what is now the U.S. state of Kentucky, which was then beyond the western borders of the Thirteen Colonies.

Books to Read

James Fenimore Cooper: *The Leatherstocking Tales*

   A series of five literary novels about the adventures of Natty Bumppo, a scout on the American frontier.

Willa Cather: *O Pioneers!*

   A classic novel written in 1913 about the physical hardships of the frontier and the enormous changes it brought to the United States.

Movies to See

Dances with Wolves

   A soldier sent to a remote western Civil War outpost makes friends with wolves and Indians.

Far and Away

   A young Irishman who loses his home after his father's death decides to go to America to begin a new life and eventually goes to live on the frontier.

Unit 6
Education in the U. S.

> Americans regard education as the means by which the inequalities among individuals are to be erased and by which every desirable end is to be achieved.
>
> —George S. Counts

Unit Goals

- To get a general knowledge of the American education system
- To get acquainted with American school life
- To identify the differences between the American education system and the Chinese education system
- To develop critical thinking and intercultural communication skills
- To learn useful words and expressions concerning the U. S. education system and improve English language skills

Before You Read

Work in small groups and discuss the topics.

1. Having been a student for more than 10 years, what have you gained from your school life?
2. Are students vessels to be filled or lamps to be lit? Which do you think is more important—learning a large quantity of facts or learning to think creatively? Why?
3. What should be the requirements for entering a university? Should extracurricular activities in high school or personal characteristics be considered?

Why, or why not?
4. What do you think are the similarities and differences between American education and Chinese education?
5. Do you recognize the saying that "the more you learn, the more you earn"? Why, or why not?

Start to Read

Text A   Education in the U. S.

The Educational Ladder

1. Americans view their public school system as an educational ladder, rising from **elementary** school to high school and finally college **undergraduate** and **graduate** programs. The educational ladder concept is an almost perfect reflection of the American ideal of individual success based on equality of opportunity and on "working your way to the top." Individuals may climb as high on the ladder as they can. The abilities of the individuals, rather than their social class, are expected to **determine** how high each person will go.

2. Most children start school at age five by attending **kindergarten**, or even at age three or four by attending preschool programs. Then usually there are six years of elementary school, two years of middle school (or junior high school), and four years of high school. School systems may divide the twelve years up differently—grouping sixth-, seventh-, and eighth-graders into middle school, for example. Not all school systems have kindergarten, but all do have twelve years of elementary, middle school, and senior high school.

3. After high school, the majority of students go on to college. Undergraduate studies lead to a **bachelor**'s degree, which is generally what Americans mean when they speak of a "college **diploma**." Students may also receive an **associate** degree for two years of study at a community college. Some of these associate degrees are in vocational or technical fields. The bachelor's degree can be followed by **professional** studies, which lead to

degrees in such professions as law and medicine, or graduate studies, which lead to master's and doctoral degrees.

School Funding Systems

4. The American public schools are free and open to all at the elementary and **secondary** (high school) level, but the public universities charge **tuition** and have competitive entrance **requirements.**

5. Although the great majority of children attend the free public elementary and high schools, about 10 percent choose to attend **private** schools. The majority of these are religious schools that are associated with particular churches and receive **financial** support from them, though parents must also pay tuition. A major purpose of these schools is to give religious **instruction**, which cannot be done in public schools, but that is not always the reason that parents send their children to Catholic or other religious schools because they believe that these schools are safer and have higher **academic** standards than the public schools.

6. There are also some elite private schools which serve mainly upper-class children. Students must pay such high tuition costs that only wealthier families can afford them, though **scholarships** are usually offered to some talented, less **affluent** children who cannot pay the tuition. Parents often send their children to these schools so that they will associate with other upper-class children and maintain the upper-class position held by their parents, in addition to getting a good education.

7. Unlike private religious schools, **elite** private schools do **conflict** with the American ideal of equal opportunity. These schools often give an extra educational and social advantage to the young people whose families have the money to allow them to attend. However, because these schools are relatively few in number, they do not displace the public schools as the central educational institution in the United States.

8. There is another area of **inequality** in the American education system. Because of the way that schools are funded, the quality of education that American students receive in public schools varies greatly. By far, the largest percentage of the money for schools comes from the local level (cities and counties), primarily from property taxes. School districts that have middle-class or wealthy families have more tax money to spend on education. Therefore, wealthier school districts have beautiful school buildings with computers and the latest science equipment, and poorer school districts have older buildings with less modern equipment.

Educating the Individual

9. American schools tend to put more **emphasis** on developing critical-thinking skills than they do on acquiring quantities of facts. American students are encouraged to ask questions, think for themselves, and express their own opinions in class, a reflection of the American values of individual freedom and self-reliance. The goal of the American education system is to teach children how to learn and to help them reach their maximum **potential**.

10. The development of social and **interpersonal** skills may be considered as important as the development of **intellectual** skills. To help students develop these other important skills, schools have added a large number of extracurricular activities to daily life at school. These activities are almost as important as the students' class work. For example, in making their decisions about which students to admit, colleges look for students who are "**well-rounded**." Grades in high school courses and scores on tests like the SAT are very important, but so are the students' **extracurricular** activities. It is by participating in these activities that students **demonstrate** their special talents, their level of **maturity** and responsibility, their leadership qualities, and their ability to get along with others.

11. Some Americans consider athletics, frequently called competitive sports, the most important of all extracurricular activities. This is because many people believe it is important for all young people, young men and young women, to learn how to compete successfully. Team sports such as football, basketball, and baseball are important because they teach students the "winning spirit." At times, the athletic competition may be carried to such an extreme that some students and their parents may place more importance on the high school's sports program than its academic offerings.

12. Student government is another extracurricular activity designed to develop competitive, political, and social skills in students. The students choose a number of student government officers who compete for the votes of their fellow students in school elections. Although these officers have little power over the central decisions of the school, the process of running for office and then taking responsibility for a number of student activities if elected is seen as good experience in developing their leadership and competitive skills, and in helping them to be responsible citizens.

13. Athletics and student government are only two of a variety of extracurricular activities found in American schools. There are clubs and activities for almost every student interest—art, music, drama, debate, foreign language, photography, volunteer work—all aimed at helping the students to become more successful in later life. Many parents watch their children's extracurricular activities with as much interest and concern as they do their children's intellectual achievements in the classroom.

After You Read

Knowledge Focus

1. Answer the following questions.
   1) What is the purpose of education?
   2) What are the major differences between public schools and private schools?
   3) Are there any areas of inequality in the American education system? Illustrate your points with instances.
   4) What other skills American schools emphasize besides intellectual skills? Why?
   5) What could be the qualities of a "well-rounded" student under American education system?

2. Choose the best answer according to the information in the text above.
   1) Which of these statements is FALSE? _____
      a. American high school students have the choice of going to a free public school or a private one where they must pay tuition.
      b. The American education system is based on strong principles of equality of opportunity—all students should have an equal opportunity to get a good education.
      c. After twelve years of school, American students receive a bachelor's degree diploma at graduation.
   2) Which of these statements is TRUE? _____
      a. Most of the money to pay for American public schools comes from local taxes.
      b. Religious schools that serve middle-class students receive money from the national government, but elite private schools do not.
      c. American schools attach the greatest importance to developing students' academic skills.

3) Which of the following would NOT be considered an extracurricular activity? _____
   a. a school baseball team
   b. the student government of a school
   c. a classroom research project

3. **Fill in the blanks according to the information in the text above.**

   1) Americans view their public school system as an educational ladder:

   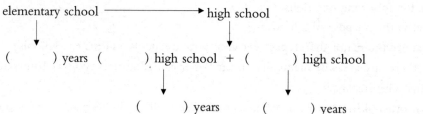

   2) Undergraduate studies lead to a _____ degree, which is generally what Americans mean when they speak of a "_____." Students may also receive a (an) _____ degree for two years of study at a community college and such degrees are usually in _____ or _____ fields.

   3) All school systems in the U.S. have twelve years of elementary, middle school, and senior high school:

   elementary school ⟶ high school

   ( ) years   ( ) high school + ( ) high school

   ( ) years   ( ) years

   4) The American public schools are _____ and _____ to all at the elementary and secondary (high school) level, but the public _____ charge tuition and have _____ entrance requirements.

   5) About 10 percent of American children choose to attend _____ schools. The majority of these are religious schools that are associated with particular _____ and receive _____ support from them.

Language Focus

1. **Match the words first and then fill in the blanks with the phrases.**

   A. entrance   a. activities
   B. intellectual   b. ladder
   C. extracurricular   c. requirements
   D. competitive   d. school
   E. well-rounded   e. degree
   F. educational   f. skill
   G. associate   g. sports
   H. elementary   h. student

1) Beach volleyball made its debut in Atlanta in 1996, but its popularity as a _____ began in the 1950s.
2) Sports and drama are the most popular _____ at school.
3) In China, children enter _____ at the age of seven, don't they?
4) Starting from 2001, the community college offers full-time _____ programs.
5) In order to meet the college _____, the students have to work very hard.
6) The educational goal of our university is to produce a great number of _____ for the society.
7) School education should attach great importance to the development of both the students' _____ and their social skills.
8) Many Americans are determined to climb to the top of the _____ and therefore they may fulfill their American dream.

2. Which word does not belong?
   There are many words in the text that have to do with education. Circle the word or phrase which does not belong in each group.
   1) kindergarten, elementary school, middle school, high school, medical school, college
   2) private, public, textbook, vocational, technical
   3) test scores, grades, extracurricular activities, local tax
   4) associate degree, bachelor's, tuition, master's, doctoral
   5) junior, freshman, athletics, sophomore, senior

3. Fill in the blanks with the proper forms of the words in the brackets.
   1) The existence of elite private schools conflicts with the American ideal of equal opportunity, which is an area of _____ (equality) in the American education system.
   2) Most children start school at age five by attending kindergarten, or even at age three or four by attending _____ (school) programs.
   3) The bachelor's degree can be followed by _____ (profession) studies, which lead to master's and doctoral degrees.
   4) American schools tend to put more _____ (emphasize) on developing critical-thinking skills than they do on acquiring quantities of facts.
   5) The development of social and _____ (personal) skills may be considered as important as the development of intellectual skills.

4. Proofreading and error correction.
   The passage contains FIVE errors. Each indicated line contains a maximum of ONE error.

In each case, only ONE word is involved.

Unrestricting by national and state standards, and created by and for the elite or particular interest groups, some private schools embrace and pursuit the same values and goals as public schools. However, they bring to the endeavor from the institutional side great resources, smaller class sizes and a greater variety of teachers (since teachers need not state-certified to teach in a private school), and they draw on and cater to a population of students which more often than not belong to the cultural elite.	1) _____ 2) _____ 3) _____ 4) _____ 5) _____

Comprehensive Work

1. Small-Group Project.

Some American parents are so dissatisfied with the public schools that they are educating their children at home. Homeschooling now provides education for an increasing number of American children, and the trend is growing rapidly. Some public school educators agree that the current model for public schools needs to be changed. Perhaps most dramatic, these alternatives to traditional public or private schools are transforming the roles of the teachers and the students, giving students more power to decide what they want to learn.

Plan an ideal school with your group. You may include these points in your description:

- Who would the students be (age, ethnicity)?
- Would the school have a special emphasis (science, music)?
- What would the teachers be like (age, experiences, roles)?
- How many students would be in a class?
- Who would determine the curriculum?
- What about tests and homework?
- How would discipline be maintained?
- What would a typical day be like?
- What special activities would the students have?

When your description is complete, share your new school with the rest of the class.

2. Essay Writing.

What do you like or dislike most about your school life in China?

Read More

Text B　　The First Day of Middle School

My stomach tied in knots, and I could feel the sweat soaking through my T-shirt. My hands were clammy as I spun the face of my combination lock. I tried and tried to remember the numbers, and every time I thought I had it, the lock wouldn't open. Around and around went the numbers, left, right, left... which way was it supposed to go? I couldn't make it work. I gave up and started to run down the hallway. As I ran, the hall seemed to get longer and longer...the door I'm trying to reach was farther away than when I had started. I began to sweat even worse, then I could feel the tears forming. I was late, for my first class on my first day of middle school. As I ran, people were watching me and they were laughing...laughing... then the bell rang! In my dream, it was the school bell. But as I sat up in bed, I realized that it was my alarm clock jarring me awake.

I was having the dream again. I started having the dream around the end of the sixth grade, and as the start of seventh grade grew closer, the more I had the dream. This time the dream was even more real, because today was the first day of seventh grade. In my heart, I knew I never would make it. Everything was too different. School, friends—even my own body.

I was used to walking to school, and now I had to walk six blocks to the bus stop so that I could take the bus to and from school. I hated buses. They made me carsick from the jiggling and the smell of the fuel.

I had to get up for school earlier than in the past, partly because of having to be bussed to school and partly because I had to take better care of myself now than I was in my preteen years. My mom told me I would have to shower every morning since my hormones were kicking in—that's why I perspired so easily.

I was totally uncomfortable with my body. My feet didn't want to respond to my own directions, and I tripped a lot. I constantly had a sprained ankle, wet armpits and things stuck in my braces. I felt awkward, smelly, insecure and like I had bad breath on a full-time basis.

In middle school, I would have to learn the rules and personalities of six different teachers instead of just one. There would be different kids in all my classes, kids I didn't even know. I had never made friends very easily, and

now I would have to start all over again.

I would have to run to my locker between classes, remembering my combination, open it, put in the books from the last class and take out different books...and make it to the next class all within five minutes!

I was also scared because of some stories I had heard about the first day of middle school, like being canned by the eighth-graders. That's when a bunch of eighth-graders pick you up and put you in a trash can. I had also heard that when eighth-grade girls catch a new seventh-grader in the girls' bathroom alone, they smear her with lipstick. Neither one of these first-day activities sounded like something I wanted to take part in.

No one had ever told me that growing up was going to be so hard, so scary, so unwelcome, so...unexpected. I was the oldest kid in my family—in fact, in my entire neighborhood—and no one had been there before me, to help lead me through the challenges of middle school. I was on my own.

The first day of school was almost everything I feared. I didn't remember my combination. I wrote the combination on my hand, but my hand was so sweaty that it came off. I was late to every class. I didn't have enough time to finish my lunch; I had just sat down to eat when the bell rang to go back to class. I almost choked on my peanut butter and jelly sandwich as I ran down the dreaded hallway. The classrooms and the teachers were a blur. I wasn't sure what teacher went with which subject and they had all assigned homework...on the very first day of school! I couldn't believe it.

But the first day wasn't like my dream in another way. In my dream, all the other kids had it together and I was the only one who was the nerd. In real life, I wasn't the only one who was late for classes. Everyone else was late, too. No one could remember their combination either, except Ted Milliken, the kid who carried a briefcase to school. After most of the kids realized that everyone else was going through the same thing they were going through, we all started cracking up. We were bumping into each other in our rush to get to the next class, and books were flying everywhere. No one got canned or smeared—at least no one I knew. I still didn't go into the girls' bathroom alone, just in case. Yeah, there was laughter in the hallway, but most of it was the laughter of kids sharing a common experience: complete hysteria!

As the weeks went by, it became easier and easier. Pretty soon I could twirl my combination without even looking at it. I hung posters in my locker, and finally felt like I was at home. I learned all my teacher's names and decided who I liked the best. Friendships from elementary school were renewed and made stronger, and new friends were made. I learned how to change into a gym suit in front of other girls. It never felt comfortable, but I did it—just like everyone else did. I don't think any of us felt very comfortable.

I still didn't like the bus; it did make me carsick. I even threw up on the bus once. (At least it was on the way home, not on the way to school.) I went to dances and parties, and I started to wonder what it would feel like to be kissed by a boy. The school had track tryouts, and I made the team and learned how to jump the low hurdles. I got pretty good at it, too.

First semester turned into second, and then third. Before I knew it, eighth grade was just around the corner. I had made it through.

Next year, on the first day of school, I would be watching the new seventh-graders sweating it out just like I did—just like everyone does. I decided that I would feel sorry for them... but only for the FIRST day of seventh grade. After that, it's a breeze.

Finish the following exercises.

1. According to the passage, in the United States, middle school starts in the _____ grade.
   a. fifth   b. sixth   c. seventh   d. eighth

2. From the passage, we know that on the first day of middle school "I" feel very _____.
   a. excited   b. scared   c. delighted   d. surprised

3. It seems there are great differences between elementary school life and middle school life. Can you find out some of the differences from "my" description?

4. My first year in middle school turns out to be _____.
   a. what "I" expected   b. going on well

Text C The Higher Learning in America: External Conditions

By Robert Maynard Hutchins

Our notion of progress is that everything is getting better and must be getting better from age to age. Our information is increasing. Our scientific knowledge is expanding. Our technological equipment in its range and excellence is far superior to what our fathers or even our older brothers knew.

Although the depression has shaken our faith a little, we still remain true to the doctrine of progress and still believe in its universal application. Politics, religion, and even education are all making progress, too. In intellectual fields, therefore, we have no hesitancy in breaking completely with the past; the ancients did not know the things we know; they had never seen steam engines, or aero-planes, or radios, and seem to have had little appreciation of the possibilities of the factory system. Since these are among the central facts in our lives, how can the ancients have anything to say to us?

Descartes, Hume, and Rousseau, for example, did not find it in the least absurd that they should begin to think as though nobody had ever thought before. They did not even regard it as egotistical. It was merely natural; mankind had progressed to the point where it was necessary to cast out old errors and begin to develop a really intelligent program.

The tremendous strides of science and technology seemed to be the result of the accumulation of data. The more information, the more discoveries, the more inventions, the more progress. The way to promote progress was therefore to get more information. The sciences one by one broke off from philosophy and then from one another, and that process is still going on. At last the whole structure of the university collapsed and the final victory of empiricism was won when the social sciences, law, and even philosophy and theology themselves became empirical and experimental and progressive.

In some way or other the theory of evolution got involved in these developments; it gave aid and comfort to empiricism and was particularly happy in its effect upon education. Evolution proves, you see, that there is steady improvement from age to age. But it shows, too, that everybody's business is to get adjusted to his environment. Obviously the way to get adjusted to the environment is to know a lot about it. And so empiricism, having taken the place of thought as the basis of research, took its place, too, as the basis of education. It led by easy stages to vocationalism; because the facts you learn about your prospective environment (particularly if you love money) ought to be as immediate and useful as possible.

We begin, then, with a notion of progress and end with an anti-intellectualism which denies, in effect, that man is a rational animal. He is an animal and perhaps somewhat more intelligent than most. As such, a man can be trained as the more intelligent animals can be. But the idea that his education should consist of the cultivation of his intellect is, of course, ridiculous. What it must consist of is surveys, more or less detailed, of the modem industrial, technological, financial, political, and social situation so that he can fit into it with a minimum of discomfort to himself and to his fellow men. Thus the modern temper produces that strangest of modern phenomena, an anti-intellectual university.

Since an anti-intellectual university is a contradiction in terms, it is no wonder that the theories justifying it are very odd. There is, for instance, the great-man theory of education. Under this theory you pay no attention to what you teach, or indeed to what you investigate. You get great men for your faculty. Their mere presence on the campus inspires, stimulates, and exalts. It matters not how inarticulate their teaching or how recondite their researches; they are, as the saying goes, an education in themselves. This is a variant of the nauseating anecdote about Mark Hopkins on one end of the log and the student on the other.

Under any conditions that are likely to exist in this country the log is too long and there are too many people sitting on both ends of it to make the anecdote apposite. Of course we should try to get great men into education, and each president should try to get as many of them as he can for his own faculty. But he can never hope to get very many, even if he knows one when he sees one. If a president succeeds in finding a few great men, he cannot hope to make them useful in an organization that ties them hand and foot and in a course of study that is going off in all directions at the same time and particularly in those opposite to the ones in which the great men are going. The fact is that the great-man theory is an excuse, an alibi, a vacuous reply to the charge that we have no intelligent program for the higher learning. It amounts to saying that we do not need one; we could give you one if we wanted to. But if you will only accept the great-man theory you will spare us the trouble of thinking.

Another theory we have developed is the character-building theory. It may be that we don't teach our students anything, but what of it? That isn't our purpose. Our purpose is to turn out well-tubbed young Americans who know how to behave in the American environment. Association with one another, with gentlemanly professors, in beautiful buildings will, along with regular exercise, make our students the kind of citizens our country needs. Since character is the result of choice it is difficult to see how you can develop it unless you train the mind to make intelligent choices. Collegiate life suggests that the choices of undergraduates are determined by other considerations than thought. Undoubtedly, fine associations, fine buildings, green grass, good food, and exercise are excellent things for anybody. You will note that they are exactly what is advertised by every resort hotel. The only reason why they are also advertised by every college and university is that we have no coherent educational program to announce.

The character-building theory turned inside out is the doctrine that every young person ought to learn to work hard; and that it is immaterial what he works at as long as he has to work. Under the theory in this form the subject matter of legal study, for example, might just as well be botany or ornithology or any subject that is of such scope and difficulty as to require a substantial amount of hard labor. The prospective lawyer would have learned to work; anything else he must learn in practice anyway.

We shall all admit, I suppose, that learning how to work is perhaps the prime requisite for a useful life. It does seem unfortunate, however, that the higher learning can contribute nothing which clerking, coal-heaving, or choir practice cannot do as well or better. It is possible that apprenticing the young in some trade from the age of fourteen on might get the result here sought after with less expense and trouble. The hard-work doctrine would seem to be a defense-mechanism set up to justify our failure to develop anything worth working on.

The great-man theory and the character-building theory amount to a denial that there is or should be content to education. Those among us who assert that there is a content to education are almost unanimous in holding that the object of the higher learning is utility, and utility in a very restricted sense. They write articles showing that the educated get better jobs and make more money. Or they advocate changes in education that will, they think, make it more effective in preparing students to get better jobs and make more money. Here we are brought back to the love of money as a cause of our confusion. As the institution's love of money makes it sensitive to every wave of popular opinion, and as the popular opinion is that insofar as education has any object it is economic, both the needs of the universities and the sentiments of the public conspire to degrade the universities into vocational schools. To these then a distorted notion of democracy leads us to admit any and all students; for should not all our youth have equal economic opportunities?

This is the position of the higher learning in America. The universities are dependent on the people. The people love money and think that education is a way of getting it. They think too that democracy means that every child should be permitted to acquire the educational insignia that will be helpful in making money. They do not believe in the cultivation of the intellect for its own sake. And the distressing part of this is that the state of the nation determines the state of education.

But how can we hope to improve the state of the nation? Only through education. A strange circularity thus afflicts us. The state of the nation depends on the state of education; but the state of education depends on the state of the nation. How can we break this vicious circle and make at last the contribution to the national life that since the earliest times has been expected of us? We can do so only if some institutions can be strong enough and clear enough to stand firm and show our people what the higher learning is. As education it is the single-minded pursuit of the intellectual virtues. As scholarship it is the single-minded devotion to the advancement of knowledge. Only if the colleges and universities can devote themselves to these objects can we look hopefully to the future of the higher learning in America.

Finish the following exercises.
1. We can infer from the passage that Hutchins is likely to disagree with the following opinions EXCEPT _____.
   A. to make progress means we should completely break with the past
   B. the way to promote progress is to get more information
   C. vocationalism should be the key point in university education
   D. a person's education should consist of the cultivation of his intellect
2. There are two theories mentioned in the passage justifying an anti-intellectual university: one is the _____ theory; the other is the _____ theory.
3. What is the essence of real education according to Hutchins?

Notes

George S. Counts (1889—1974) was an American educator and influential education theorist. Counts is credited for influencing several subsequent theories, particularly critical pedagogy. Counts wrote dozens of important papers and 29 books about education. He was also highly active in politics as a leading advocate of teachers' unions, the head of the American Federation of Teachers, the founder of the New York State Liberal Party, and as a candidate for the U.S. Senate.

Books to Read

Robert Maynard Hutchins: ***The Higher Learning in America***

A call for Americans to muster the imagination and courage to get education for their country before it is too late.

Allan Bloom: ***The Closing of the American Mind***

How higher education has failed democracy and impoverished the souls of today's students in the U.S.

Mike Rose: ***Lives on the Boundary***

A teacher in the inner city describes his innovative methods for teaching children and adults who are educationally disadvantaged.

Leonard Q. Ross: ***The Education of Hyman Kaplan***

The humorous story of an immigrant's attempt to learn English and become an American.

Movies to See

Music of the Heart

The story of a schoolteacher's struggle to teach violin to inner-city children in New York City's Harlem.

The Ron Clark Story

Based on the true story of Ron Clark, an inspiring tale of an energetic, creative and idealistic young teacher who leaves his small North Carolina hometown to teach in a public school in New York City's Harlem.

Unit 7
Government and Politics in the U. S.

> A wise and frugal Government shall restrain men from injuring one another, [and] shall leave them otherwise free to regulate their own pursuits of industry and improvements.
> —Thomas Jefferson

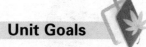
Unit Goals

- To get a general knowledge of American constitution and the federal system
- To be aware of American people's understanding about government
- To learn how American political system works in reality
- To learn some political terms on government and politics in the United States
- To develop critical thinking and intercultural communication skills
- To learn useful words and expressions concerning the American government and improve English language skills

Before You Read

1. Preview vocabulary.

   Read the quotation and find the words with the following meanings. Write each word next to its meaning.

   _____ 1) the act of trying to get something

   _____ 2) prevent someone from doing something

   _____ 3) to control the activity by rules

   _____ 4) hurting

2. Work with your partner and consider the following questions.

1) Do you agree with the quotation by Thomas Jefferson? Paraphrase the quotation in your own words.
2) How do you understand the statement "Government is a necessary evil"?
3) What are the two major political parties in the United States? What is the main difference in their beliefs?
4) What personal qualities do you think political leaders should have?

3. Recognize the following Presidents in American history.

Who are the Presidents?
Tell your classmates what you know about them.

Start to Read

Text A   The Organization of the American Government

A Suspicion of Strong Government

1. The ideal of the free individual has had a **profound** effect on the way Americans view their government. Traditionally, there has been a deep **suspicion** that government is the natural enemy of freedom, even if it is elected by the people. The bigger and stronger the government becomes, the more dangerous many Americans believe it is to their individual freedom.

2. This suspicion of strong government goes back to the men who led the American Revolution in 1776. These men believed the government of Great Britain wanted to discourage the freedom and economic opportunities of the

American colonists by excessive taxes and other measures which would ultimately benefit the British aristocracy and monarchy. Thomas Paine, the famous revolutionary writer, expressed the view of other American revolutionists when he said, "Government even in its best state is but a necessary evil; in its worst state, an **intolerable** one." In fact, the way in which the national government is organized in the U. S. Constitution provides an excellent illustration of the American suspicion of governmental power.

The Constitution

3. The Constitution of the United States was adopted on June 21, 1788. It is the oldest written constitution still in use. What is the Constitution? It is the basic law from which the U. S. government gets all its power. It is the law that protects those who live in the U. S. from unreasonable actions by the national government or any state government.

4. The Constitution defines three branches of government. They are the **legislative** branch, which enacts laws; the **executive** branch, which enforces those laws; and the **judicial** branch, which **interprets** them.

5. The legislative branch is called **Congress**. It is made up of two groups of legislators—the Senate and the House of **Representatives**. A member of the Senate is addressed as **Senator**. Members of the House of Representatives are called congressmen or congresswomen. The Senate is often referred to as the upper house. It has 100 members—two senators from each state. Both senators represent the entire state. Senators are elected for six-year terms. Every two years, one-third of all senators face reelection.

6. The lower house, which is called the House of Representatives, has 435 members, all of whom are elected every two years. The number of representatives from each state is determined by that state's population. While the seven smallest states have only one representative each, California, the most **populous** state, has 53 representatives in the 117th Congress (2021—2022). For the purpose of electing representatives, each state is divided into congressional districts. The districts within a state are about equal in population. One representative is elected from each district. One of a representative's major duties is to protect the interests of the people in that district.

7. The job of Congress is to pass laws. Before a law is passed, it is called a bill. In order to become a law, a bill must be approved by a majority of each house of Congress and by the president. If the president **vetoes** a bill, it can still become law if at least two-thirds of the members of each house of Congress **override** the veto by voting for it when it is voted on again.

8. The president is the nation's chief executive. As such, he must see that all national laws are carried out. The president also spends much of his time making decisions about foreign policy. Of course, a very large staff of advisers and other employees assist the president. The most important group of advisers is called the **cabinet**. The cabinet consists of the heads of the 14 departments of the executive branch, such as the Secretaries of Education, Defense and Agriculture. Cabinet members are chosen by the president with the **approval** of the Senate. The president also appoints ambassadors and other consular heads who represents the U.S. abroad. In addition, he appoints judges of the **federal** courts.

9. The vice president is the only other elected person in the executive branch. One important constitutional duty of the person holding this office is to serve as president of the Senate. The vice president's most important function is to become president upon the death, resignation, or disability of the president. Out of 46 presidents elected, eight have died in office, and one **resigned**. In each case, the vice president became president.

10. The judicial branch consists of the federal courts, including the highest court of the U.S., the Supreme Court. One of the unusual features of the American judicial system is the power of the courts to declare legislation **unconstitutional** and, therefore, **void**. The power of the federal government is limited by the Constitution. Federal laws cannot **violate** the terms of the Constitution.

11. Federal laws are in some way controlled or affected by all three branches of government—Congress makes them; the president approves and enforces them; and the courts determine what they mean and whether they are constitutional. Each branch of government prevents improper actions by the other branches; if any one of the three branches starts to abuse its power, the other two may join together to stop it.

After You Read

Knowledge Focus

1. **Fill in this graphic organizer with information about how the U.S. government is organized.** First write the names of the three branches of government. Then write what the members are in each branch. Finally, write what the responsibilities are for each branch.

Branch	Institutions and Members	Responsibilities
Executive	(　　) Cabinet	(　　)
(　　)	Congress Senate (　　) House (　　)	make laws
(　　)	Supreme Court (　　)	(　　)

2. **Put a tick (√) in the correct column for each job listed.**
   Who's elected? Who's appointed?

Government Employees	Elected	Appointed
the president		
the cabinet		
the vice president		
senators		
federal judges		

3. Choose the best answer according to the information in the text.

1) Americans do not want to have a strong national government because _____.
   a. they are afraid of their political leaders
   b. they are afraid it will put limits on their individual freedom
   c. they are much more concerned with national glory
   d. they are strong enough to build one

2) The Constitution of the United States _____.
   a. gives by far the most power to congress
   b. gives by far the most power to the president
   c. gives by far the most power to the supreme court
   d. tries to give each branch enough power to balance the others

3) In the U.S., the president can _____ a bill from Congress, but the bill can still become law if at least _____ of the members in each house vote for it when it is voted on again.
   a. void, 2/3
   b. veto, 1/3
   c. veto, 2/3
   d. void, 1/3

Language Focus

1. Complete the following sentences with the proper key vocabulary word.

   | veto | representative | unconstitutional |
   | interpret | congress | senator | federal |

   1) One of the jobs of the Supreme Court is to _____ the Constitution.
   2) In a(n) _____ system of government, the governing powers are divided between the state government and the national government.
   3) If Congress votes in favor of making a bill a law, the president can still stop that bill from becoming law by using the _____ power.
   4) Every state elects two _____ to the Upper House, but in the Lower House, the number of _____ from each state varies, depending on the state's population.
   5) The House of Representatives and the Senate together make up _____.
   6) When a law violates the U.S. Constitution, the judicial branch of government will declare it _____.

2. **Which word does not belong?**

   This text contains a number of words that have to do with government and politics. Look at each group of words, and decide which one does not belong with the boldfaced word.

   Underline the word which does not belong with the boldfaced word.

   EXAMPLE: **parties**: Republican, Democrat, <u>FBI</u>

   1) **executive branch**: president, cabinet, congress, policy, veto, vice president
   2) **legislative branch**: Congress, Supreme Court, Senate, House of Representatives, bill
   3) **judicial branch**: federal courts, Supreme Court, judges, secretary of Defense

3. **Proofreading and error correction.**

   The passage contains FIVE errors. Each indicated line contains a maximum of ONE error. In each case, only ONE word is involved.

Since this period, the Democratic Party has took on the role of the liberal party the closest major party equivalent to the labor parties of Europe. The party has traditionally aligned itself with labor unions and the working class. It is generally supported the expansion of civil rights and a woman's right to choose an abortion, as well the traditional provisions of the welfare state. The Republican Party on the one hand, supports the expansion of the free market economy and the dismantling of the welfare state. It has generally opposed to a woman's right to an abortion and has worked to promote traditional religion through government.	1) _____ 2) _____ 3) _____ 4) _____ 5) _____

Comprehensive Work

1. **Interpret the following government quotes.**

   How do you interpret the following quotes on government? Do you agree with the statements? Work with your partners and share your understandings with each other.

   ● We hang the petty thieves and appoint the great ones to public office.

   —**Aesop**

- By definition, a government has no conscience. Sometimes it has a policy, but nothing more.

  —**Albert Camus**

- A nation of sheep will beget a government of wolves.

  —**Edward R. Murrow**

- A nation that is afraid to let its people judge the truth and falsehood in an open market is a nation that is afraid of its people.

  —**John F. Kennedy**

- The care of human life and happiness, and not their destruction, is the first and only object of good government.

  —**Thomas Jefferson**

2. **Group-project:** Work with your team members to discuss the following topic.

   What are the advantages and disadvantages of the U.S. government organization?

Advantages	Disadvantages

3. **Essay Writing.**

   What makes a good government?

Read More

Text B Why Not a Parliament?

By Donald A. Ritchie

Some of the ideas discarded at the constitutional convention might have created a legislative branch closer to a parliament, where the prime minister and cabinet secretaries are members of the legislature. Congress might have elected presidents and might have been able to remove them for "maladministration," provisions that could have turned the presidency into something closer to a prime minister, with tenure dependent on retaining the majority in Congress. There were even suggestions that senators serve for life, at no pay, making the Senate a House of Lords, with the House of Representatives as the House of Commons.

Nevertheless, Congress did follow the British Parliament's bicameral model. For more than a century, colonial legislatures had generally been divided between an upper house, or governor's council, and a popularly elected assembly. During the American Revolution, some of the states abolished their upper houses, regarding single-body legislatures as more egalitarian. The Continental Congress and the Congress under the Articles of Confederation were also single bodies. Property holders, however, worried that unchecked democratic legislatures would turn confiscatory, and that way of thinking added extra layers to the Constitution. Whereas representatives would be directly elected by people, senators initially would be elected by the state legislatures, and the Electoral College would choose the president, forming a mixed government to prevent an "excess of democracy."

The U.S. government distinctly differs from parliamentary democracies. Neither the president nor the cabinet secretaries sit in Congress, and no member of any branch can serve simultaneously in another (except for the vice president, whom the Constitution installed as president of the Senate to keep him occupied until and unless he was needed to fill a vacancy in the presidency). Unlike prime ministers, American presidents do not lose office if their party's majority falls in the next congressional elections. So presidents have frequently had to contend with congressional majorities led by the opposition.

The BBC correspondent Alistair Cooke observed that British ambassadors to the United States were invariably puzzled about why there was no "question period" where Congress could quiz presidents on current policies the way the House of Commons questions prime ministers. Cooke explained to them that while separation of the branches prevented this, Congress had the advantage of being able to call the president's cabinet for scrutiny before its committees. He argued that the questions and guffaws that prime ministers and cabinet officers faced in the British House of Commons could not be compared, "as a form of executive torture, to an all-day inquisition by a standing committee of Congress." Without the support of a parliamentary majority, the prime minister's government falls, but congressional majorities can ignore the president's legislative proposals, reject his budget, refuse to confirm his nominees, and decline to approve treaties his administration has negotiated.

Party discipline in Congress ebbs and flows over time, and varies between the House and Senate, but in general it is rarely as strong as in a parliamentary system. Senators and representatives hold themselves accountable first and foremost to their constituents. Party leaders have trouble retaliating against dissidents whose votes they will be courting on the next issue. The majority leader may need to appeal to members of the opposition to win a vote. Conversely, congressional leaders rarely need worry about third parties or forge coalitions to govern, as happens in parliamentary systems, since none of the states practice proportional representation to help smaller parties gain seats in Congress. Even the physical setting differs. Unlike most parliaments, where the major parties hector each other while directly facing each other, the semicircular seating in the House and Senate chambers facilitates, at times, bipartisan alliances.

Other democracies overwhelmingly prefer a parliamentary system. The U.S. Congress, by contrast, is slower, more cumbersome, and less efficient—but that was what the framers of the Constitution intended. They designed a system to resist hasty action and temper any sudden shifts in public opinion, to prevent undue concentration of power, to protect citizens' rights, and to forge a national consensus on demanding issues.

Finish the following exercises.
1. What are the major differences between a parliament and U.S. Congress?
2. How does the U.S. government differ from parliamentary democracies?
3. What is the purpose of choosing Congress instead of a parliament?
4. Mark each statement True or False:
    a. American presidents are elected by the U.S. Congress. _____
    b. Senators in the U.S. Congress serve for life. _____
    c. The U.S. Congress followed the British Parliament's bicameral model. _____
    d. Neither the president nor the cabinet secretaries sit in the U.S. Congress, and in fact no member of any branch serves simultaneously in another. _____
    e. Prime ministers lose office if their party's majority falls in the next parliamentary elections. _____
    f. Senators and representatives hold themselves accountable first and foremost to their constituents. _____
    g. The U.S. Congress is slower, more cumbersome, and less efficient than a parliament. _____

Text C The Triumph of Technology

The American presidential election of 2000 was, to put it mildly, controversial. People still argue over whether George Bush truly won in Florida, the state whose electoral votes made him president even though he had garnered fewer votes nationwide than Al Gore, his main opponent.

The presidential election in November, 2004 was of crucial importance—and once again, observers generally agreed, very close. In addition, the Senate was split 51 – 49 in favor of the Republicans, so a shift of only two seats could either hand it to the Democrats or make it much likelier to cooperate with a right-wing Republican president. How can an accurate vote count be guaranteed?

It cannot, at least not in an absolute sense. All voting systems are open to tampering and error. The earliest elections to audit are the least technically sophisticated: voting with paper ballots. However, ballot boxes can be "stuffed"—and occasionally have been in America, in cities or counties under the control of one tightly disciplined and unscrupulous political organization. Today oversight committees and the press make the stuffing of ballot boxes far less likely, as do private polls of people leaving voting stations: if the polls produce different results from the balloting, then something is fishy.

Why all this fuss with papers, pens and ballot boxes when machines can simplify the whole task? Actually, the trouble in Florida centered on the difficulty of reading ballots from voting machines. Ah, but we live in a high-tech era: why not go over to electronic voting using touch-screen systems or the Internet? Because these electronic methods are far more open to manipulation, whether by mischief-minded hackers or political operatives who will stop at nothing to win. And if tampering occurs, a clean audit of the votes is impossible.

Who knows what could happen if an irresponsible young fool hacked into voting system? Nervous Democrats, however, have noticed two disquieting things about companies that produce voting technology: their security precautions are inexcusably sloppy—and the firms are mostly controlled by businessmen allied with the Republican Party.

Finish the following exercises.

1. The two major political parties in the United States are _____ Party & _____ Party.
2. "All voting systems are open to tampering and error." The statement carries the meaning that the voting systems are _____ (likely / unlikely) to be abused.
3. "If the polls produce different results from the balloting, then something is fishy." The word "fishy" here means _____.
   a. questionable   b. reasonable   c. reliable

4. According to the article, the electronic voting system is a _____ (good / bad) choice.
5. In the United States, the interests of the businessmen are usually represented by the _____ Party.

Notes

1. **Thomas Paine** (1737—1809) was an English pamphleteer, revolutionary, radical, inventor and intellectual. His main contribution was as the author of the powerful, widely read pamphlet, *Common Sense* (1776), advocating independence for the American Colonies from the Kingdom of Great Britain.

2. **Al Gore** (1948—) is an American environmental activist, author, public intellectual, businessperson, former politician, and former journalist. He served as the forty-fifth Vice President of the United States from 1993 to 2001 under President Bill Clinton. In 2007, Gore was awarded the Nobel Peace Prize.

For Fun

Book to Read
Kelvin Phillips: *American Dynasty: Aristocracy, Fortune, and the Politics of Deceit in the House of Bush*
   A controversial book that traces how the Bush family rose to power.

Movies and TV Series to See
House of Cards
   A Congressman works with his equally conniving wife to exact revenge on the people who betrayed him.

The West Wing
An American television serial drama that provides a glimpse into presidential politics in the nation's capital as it tells the stories of the members of a fictional presidential administration.

Unit 8
The U. S. —A Nation of Nations

> So in this continent, the energy of Irish, Germans, Swedes, Poles and all the European tribes, of the Africans, and of the Polynesians—will construct a new race, a new religion, a new state.
>
> —Ralph Waldo Emerson

Unit Goals

- To get a general knowledge of the diverse cultures of the U. S.
- To learn the effects of immigration in the U. S.
- To recognize the U. S. as a universal nation
- To develop critical thinking and intercultural communication skills
- To learn useful words and expressions concerning ethnical diversity of the U. S. and improve English language skills

Before You Read

Preview vocabulary.

1. Here are some key words in this unit. Look at their definitions. Put a check to the words you already know.

    _____ 1) *ethnic*   of a race or a particular cultural group
    _____ 2) *diversity*   the condition of being different from one another
    _____ 3) *assimilate*   become a part of another social group or state
    _____ 4) *distinct*   different in kind, separate
    _____ 5) *adopt*   take somebody into one's family as a relation

2. Work with a partner. Complete each question with a word from the proceeding list. Then answer the questions.

1) Many people of the world emigrate from their home countries to the United States. Can we say that the United States is the _____ country of the immigrants?

2) Are there any minority _____ groups in China? How many?

3) Why do some immigrants want to _____ quickly into the new culture?

4) Is racial _____ a good thing to the development of the country?

5) If some day you emigrate from your home country to a foreign country, do you still want to keep the _____ features of your home culture?

Start to Read

Text A　　The U. S.—A Nation of Nations

The Assimilation

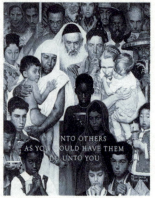

1. As is the case in many cultures, the degree to which a **minority** group was seen as different from the characteristics of the **dominant majority** determined the extent of that group's acceptance. Although **immigrants** who were like the earlier settlers were accepted, those with significantly different characteristics tended to be viewed as a threat to traditional American values and way of life.

2. This was particularly true of the immigrants who arrived by millions during the late nineteenth and early twentieth centuries. Most of them came from **poverty-stricken** nations of southern and eastern Europe. They spoke languages other than English, and large numbers of them were Catholics or Jews.

3. Americans at the time were very fearful of this new flood of immigrants. They were afraid that these people were so **accustomed** to lives of poverty and dependence that they would not understand such traditional American values as self-reliance and competition. There were so many new immigrants that they might even change the basic values of the nation in **undesirable** ways.

4. Americans tried to meet what they saw as a threat to their values by offering English instruction for the new immigrants and citizenship classes to teach them basic American beliefs. The immigrants, however, often felt that

92

their American teachers **disapproved** of the traditions of their homeland. Moreover, learning about American values gave them little help in meeting their most important needs, such as employment, food, and a place to live.

5. Far more helpful to the new immigrants were the "political bosses" of the larger cities of the northeastern United States, where most of the immigrants first arrived. Those bosses saw to many of the practical needs of the immigrants and were more accepting of the different homeland traditions. In **exchange** for their help, the bosses expected the immigrants to keep them in power by voting for them in elections.

6. Many Americans strongly disapproved of the political bosses. This was partly because the bosses were frequently **corrupt**; that is, they often stole money from the city governments they controlled and engaged in other **illegal** practices. Perhaps more important to disapproving Americans, however, was the fact that the bosses seemed to be destroying such basic American values as self-reliance and competition.

7. Despite these criticisms, many scholars believe that the political bosses performed an important function in the late nineteenth and early twentieth centuries. They helped to **assimilate** large numbers of new immigrants into the larger American culture by finding them jobs and housing, in return for their political support.

8. The fact that the United States had a rapidly **expanding** economy at the turn of the 20th century made it possible for these new immigrants, often with the help of the bosses, to **better** their standard of living in the United States. As a result of these new opportunities and new rewards, immigrants came to accept most of the values of the larger American culture and were in return accepted by the great majority of Americans.

Melting Pot or Salad Bowl

9. The population of the United States includes a large variety of **ethnic** groups coming from many races, nationalities, and religions. The process by which these many groups have been made a part of a common cultural life with commonly shared values is called **assimilation**. Scholars disagree as to the extent to which assimilation has occurred in the United States. Some have described the United States as a "melting pot" where various racial and ethnic groups have been **combined** into one culture. Others are **inclined** to see the United States as a "salad bowl" where the various groups have remained somewhat **distinct** and different from one another, creating a richly **diverse**

country.

10. The truth probably lies somewhere between these two views. Since 1776, an enormous amount of racial and ethnic assimilation has taken place in the United States, yet some groups continue to feel a strong sense of separateness from the culture as a whole. Many of these groups are really **bicultural**. That is, they consider themselves Americans, but they may also wish to **retain** the language and sometimes the cultural traditions of their **original** culture.

11. Perhaps the United States will be described not as a "melting pot or a salad bowl," but as a "mosaic"—a picture made up of many tiny pieces of different colors. If one looks closely at the nation, the individuals of different colors and ethnic groups are still distinct and recognizable, but together they create a picture that is **uniquely** American. As a nation which is **composed** of many, the **motto** for the United States is "Out of many, one."

Contributions of Immigrants

12. The wide **variety** of immigrant groups in the U.S. has given the nation great **diversity** in its industrial development. Germans, Scandinavians, and Poles share the **credit** for turning millions of acres of wilderness into farmland. Scandinavians and Canadians helped to develop the lumber industry. The Swedes built the first log cabins. The Swiss brought clock-making and cheese-making skills. The English were experienced in the handling of horses, cattle, and sheep. The Greeks, Italians, Portuguese, and Spanish grew citrus fruits and grapes. Italians started the wine industry. Chinese and Irish laborers built the first railroad that spanned the nation.

13. In addition to their skills, immigrants brought their political and social theories, religions, academic traditions, holidays, festivals, sports, arts, hobbies, and foods. The Germans introduced the Christmas tree, kindergarten, and the symphony orchestra. The Dutch brought ice-skating, bowling, golf, and the art of growing tulips. The French taught Americans elegant European cooking and dancing. Italians brought their talents in painting, sculpture, and architecture. The Irish established the Catholic Church as an English-speaking institution, introduced parochial schools, and built many Catholic colleges.

14. The American diet has also been delightfully affected by various immigrant groups. The Dutch taught Americans to make waffles and doughnuts.

The Germans brought hamburgers and sausages. Italians introduced pizza, spaghetti, minestrone, and ravioli. Americans also enjoy Swiss cheeses and fondue, Irish stew, Chinese chow mein, Indian curries, Russian caviar, Middle Eastern shish kebab, Danish pastry, French chocolate mousse, and Turkish coffee.

15. In spite of the nation's immigrant tradition, it is still not easy being a newcomer to the U. S. Often, there is family **conflict** because parents hold onto "old-country" ways while their children become Americanized. For many adult immigrants, learning English is a very difficult task. Finding a good job in this highly technological nation is another challenge. Nevertheless, most immigrants love their **adopted** land and live happily in it. They have **enriched** their adopted land with their skills, talents, ideas, and hard work.

After You Read

Knowledge Focus

1. Put a tick (√) in the correct column.
   Who should take the credit?

Contributions	Germans	English	Swiss	Italians	Irish	Chinese
introduced clock-making skills						
brought hamburgers and sausages						
built the first nationwide railroad						
started the wine industry						
introduced parochial schools						
experienced in the handling of horses, cattle, and sheep						
introduced the Christmas tree, kindergarten						

2. **Answer the following questions.**

1) Why were Americans very fearful of this new flood of immigrants in the late nineteenth and early twentieth century?

2) How did those "political bosses" help those immigrants? Why did many Americans strongly disapprove of the political bosses?

3) What are the differences between the terms "Melting Pot," "Salad Bowl" and "Mosaic"?

4) What are the contributions that the immigrants have made to the United States?

Language Focus

1. **Complete the following sentences with the proper word.**

minority	credit	dominant	majority
poverty-stricken	corrupt	better (v.)	variety
combine	retain		

1) It's safe to say that China is a _____ country in the sport of diving in the world.

2) Our country should give aids to the _____ areas and help them improve their economic conditions.

3) The performance was a tremendous success and for this the excellent players must take full _____.

4) I hate the boring life I'm living now, and I want to have _____ in my life.

5) She was elected president by a _____ of 52.

6) Many policies have been established to _____ the living conditions of the migrant workers.

7) Do you still _____ the custom of praying before you go to bed?

8) Let's _____ our efforts against our competitors.

2. **Use the following expressions to complete the sentences.**

accustom to	disapprove of	see to
hold onto	to (some) extent	be/feel inclined to
be composed of	in exchange for	

1) I don't _____ work today, for I am low with a cold.

2) Many people _____ experimenting on animals. They think it's too cruel.

3) Our economic development has been affected by the financial crisis _____, but not very seriously.

4) Will you please _____ my dog while I'm away on business?

5) There are some people who _____ their jobs long after they should have retired.

6) It takes time for newcomers to _____ the life here.

7) The little mermaid sold her voice to the wicked witch _____ the legs.

8) The university _____ five colleges and one graduate school.

3. **Fill in the blanks with the proper forms of the words in the brackets.**
   1) There were so many new immigrants that they might even change the basic values of the nation in _____ (desirable) ways.
   2) The process by which these many groups have been made a part of a common cultural life with commonly shared values is called _____ (assimilate).
   3) The immigrants, however, often felt that their American teachers _____ (approve) of the traditions of their homeland.
   4) The political bosses often stole money from the city governments they controlled and engaged in other _____ (legal) practices.
   5) Immigrants may also wish to retain the language and sometimes the cultural traditions of their _____ (origin) culture.
   6) In return, immigrants have _____ (rich) their adopted land with their skills, talents, ideas, and hard work.
   7) The wide _____ (vary) of immigrant groups in the U. S. has given the nation great _____ (diverse) in its industrial development.

4. **Proofreading and error correction.**
   The passage contains FIVE errors. Each indicated line contains a maximum of ONE error. In each case, only ONE word is involved.

   The United States is traditionally defined as a nation of immigrant. Images of poor, huddled masses welcome by the Statue of Liberty just prior to disembarkation at Ellis Island and visions of a "melting-pot" assimilate new arrivals dominate public symbolism of this past. These characterizations, furthermore, hide other histories of the country's immigrant past, including the discriminatory use of quotas to exclude certain groups and the potent forces of nativism made many feel unwelcome after arrival. The benevolent image of immigration veils yet another history of the forced immigration of African Americans from Africa into slavery.

   1) _____
   2) _____
   3) _____
   4) _____
   5) _____

Comprehensive Work

1. **Work in groups of four and share ideas with your team members.**
   Discuss the issues in small groups.
   1) People used to talk about immigrants assimilation. Now, Americans talk about accepting and appreciating the customs of immigrants.
      A. In what areas of life do you think immigrants should assimilate?
      B. In what areas should they retain the customs and lifestyles of their native country?
   2) If you ever decide to move to another country, which country would you choose and why?

2. **Essay Writing.**
   What do you think will happen to the world in the age of accelerating globalization? Will it become a salad bowl or a melting pot?

Read More

Text B — The History of Chinese Americans

Read the following passage, and then summarize "The History of Chinese Americans" in your own words.

For many years, it was common in the United States to associate Chinese Americans with restaurants and laundries. People did not realize that the Chinese had been driven into these occupations by the prejudice and discrimination that faced them in the country.

The first Chinese to reach the United States came during the California Gold Rush of 1849. Like most of the other people there, they had come to search for gold. In that largely unoccupied land, the men staked a claim for themselves by placing markers in the ground. However, either because the Chinese were so different from the others or because they worked so patiently that they sometimes succeeded in turning a seemingly worthless mining claim into a profitable one; they became the scapegoats of their envious competitors. They were harassed in many ways. Often they were prevented from working their claims; some localities even passed regulations forbidding them to own claims. The Chinese, therefore, started to seek out other ways of earning a living. Some of them began to do the laundry for the white miners; others set up small restaurants. Some went to work as farmhands or as fishermen.

In the early 1860s, many more Chinese arrived in California. This time the men were imported as work crews to construct the first transcontinental railroad. They were sorely needed because the work was so strenuous and dangerous, and it was carried on in such a remote part of the country that the railroad company could not find other laborers for the job. As in the case of their predecessors, these Chinese were almost all males; and like them, too, they encountered a great deal of prejudice. The hostility grew especially strong after the railroad project was complete, and the imported laborers returned to California—thousands of them, all out of work. Because there were so many more of them this time, these Chinese drew even more attention than the earlier group did. They were so very different in every respect: in their physical appearance, including a long "pigtail" at the back of their otherwise shaved heads, in the strange non-Western clothes they wore, in their speech, and in their religion.

When times were hard, they were blamed for working for lower wages and taking jobs away from white men, who were in many cases recent immigrants themselves. Anti-Chinese riots broke out in several cities, culminating in arson and bloodshed. Chinese were barred from using the courts and also from becoming American citizens. Californians began to demand that no more Chinese be permitted to enter their state. Finally, in 1882, they persuaded Congress to pass the Chinese Exclusion Act, which stopped the immigration of Chinese laborers. Many Chinese returned to their homeland, and their numbers declined sharply in the early part of the 20th century. However, during the World War II, when China was an ally of the United States, the Exclusion laws were ended; a small number of Chinese were allowed to immigrate each year, and Chinese could become American citizens. In 1965, many more Chinese were permitted to settle in the country, as discrimination against Asian immigration was abolished.

From the start, the Chinese had lived apart in their own separate neighborhoods, which came to be known as "Chinatowns." In each of them, the residents organized an unofficial government to make rules for the community and to settle disputes. Unable to find jobs outside, many went into business for

themselves—primarily to serve their own neighborhood. As for laundries and restaurants, some of them soon spread to other parts of the city, since such services continued to be in demand among non-Chinese, too. To this day, certain Chinatowns, especially those of San Francisco and New York, are busy, thriving communities, which have become great attractions for tourists and for those who enjoy Chinese food.

Chinese Americans retain many aspects of their ancient culture, even after having lived in the U.S. for several generations. For example, their family ties continue to be remarkably strong. Members of the family lend each other moral support and also practical help when necessary. From a very young age children are imbued with the old values and attitudes, including respect for their elders and a feeling of responsibility for the family. This helps to explain why there is so little juvenile delinquency among them.

The high regard for education which is deeply imbedded in Chinese culture and the willingness to work very hard to gain advancement, are other noteworthy characteristics of theirs. This explains why so many descendants of uneducated laborers have succeeded in becoming doctors, lawyers, and other professionals.

Chinese Americans make up only a tiny fraction of the population; there are fewer than half a million, living chiefly in California, New York, and Hawaii. As American attitudes toward minorities and toward ethnic differences have changed in recent years, the long-reviled Chinese have gained wide acceptance. Today, they are generally admired for their many remarkable characteristics, and are often held up as an example worth following. And their numerous contributions to their adopted land are much appreciated.

Text C African-American

A notable term "African-American" was often heard during news reports and interviews on the radio and television. However, not all Americans, including the blacks, have received the term "African-American" with enthusiasm. When Ann Landers, a well-known newspaper columnist, applauded for the term in her column, she was stunned by the responses from the general public. "A huge number of readers of all races wrote to say that they do not approve of the designation African-American," admitted Ann Landers in one of her later columns.

A black woman from Alabama was apparently irritated by her term. In the letter to Ms. Landers, she wrote: I am black. I have never seen Africa. My parents have never seen Africa. My grandparents have never seen Africa. My great-grandparents have never seen Africa. Why would I want to be called African-American?

It is a known fact that America is a "melting pot" in terms of its people, culture, customs and family blood lines. The majority of Americans have mixed blood in their veins, and the blacks are no exception. Since blacks achieved their freedom, there have been inter-marriages among blacks with other ethnic groups. Therefore, it is not fair to generalize that all the American blacks have their roots in Africa. A person from Missouri regards the term "African-American" as nothing but unrealistic. He impatiently pointed out: if we go that route, I'd have to be called Scotch-Irish, Polish-Hungarian-American. Who needs all those labels? How about just American? A New Jersey resident clearly stated his opinion: Blacks have been in this country for over 200 years. They are just as American as any other ethnic group. Why dilute their prestige by designating the continent of their ancestors? It is counter-productive.

The argument over "African-American" has involved other minority groups as well. Someone from Seattle wrote to the newspaper: I could never understand why people whose ancestors came from Africa allowed themselves to be called black. My grandparents came from Japan, and I would be offended if someone called me "yellow." To identify a person by color is just plain insulting.

The American Indians, however, approached this issue with a different tone. One of them confronted the newspaper columnist with the following words: You gave a lot of space to the African-American. I wish you'd do as much for the Native American Indian. We are the most ignored of all the minorities. They don't call us anything and nobody cares. The treatment of our people is the darkest page in America's history. America was our country, and now America wants no part of us.

What will finally come out of this argument about "African-American"? Nobody can offer any insightful suggestion yet. Nevertheless, it is not hard to see the regret in Ann Landers' tone when she told her readers that she "stepped on a land mine" by demonstrating her favor of the term "African-American."

Consider the following questions.
1. How did different people react differently to the term "African-American"?
2. What do you know about the history of African-Americans in the U.S.?
3. What famous African-Americans can you name? Why are they famous?

Proper Names

Scandinavian	adj.	斯堪的纳维亚(包括挪威、瑞典、丹麦、冰岛)的,斯堪的纳维亚人的
	n.	斯堪的纳维亚人,斯堪的纳维亚语
Portuguese	adj.	葡萄牙的,葡萄牙人的,葡萄牙语的
	n.	葡萄牙人,葡萄牙语
San Francisco	n.	旧金山(美国加利福尼亚州西部港口城市)
Hawaii	n.	夏威夷(美国州名)
Alabama	n.	阿拉巴马(美国州名)
Missouri	n.	密苏里(美国州名)
New Jersey	n.	新泽西(美国州名)
Seattle	n.	西雅图(美国华盛顿州港口城市)

Notes

Ralph Waldo Emerson (1803—1882) was an American essayist, philosopher, poet, and leader of the Transcendentalist movement in the early 19th century. His teachings directly influenced the growing New Thought movement of the mid 1800s.

For Fun

Books to Read

Donna Jackson Nakazawa: *Does Anybody Else Look Like Me? A Parents' Guide to Raising Multiracial Children*

　　A psychological guide to help multiracial children of all ages develop confidence and a healthy sense of self.

Ronald Takaki: *Strangers from a Different Shore*

　　The author presents a history of Asian Americans using personal experiences mixed with historical facts.

Movies to See

The Color Purple

    The hard life and painful experiences of a young African-American woman living in the South.

My Big Fat Greek Wedding

    A young Greek woman falls in love with a non-Greek and struggles to get her family to accept him while she comes to terms with her heritage and cultural identity.

Unit 9
Love and Marriage in the U.S.

> Marriage halves our griefs, doubles our joys, and quadruples our expenses.
> —Anonymous

Unit Goals

- To get to know love and marriage of American styles
- To learn some customs concerning American wedding
- To develop critical thinking and intercultural communication skills
- To learn some words and expressions concerning American dating patterns and wedding and improve English language skills

Before You Read

1. Here are some popular sayings about love and marriage. How do you understand the sayings?

   1) Marry in haste, repent at leisure.
   2) Love is blind.
   3) Beauty is in the eye of the beholder.
   4) Let your heart rule your head.
   5) Wear your heart on your sleeve.

2. What is LOVE? Define it in your own way.
   LOVE is _____

Start to Read

Text A   Marriage: American Style

Before the Wedding

1. Although Americans try to be practical in most matters, when they choose a spouse, the decision is usually based upon feelings of love rather than on practical **considerations**. In the U.S., parents do not arrange marriages for their children. Teenagers usually begin dating in high school and eventually find partners through their own social contacts. They want to "fall in love" before they think about marriage. Most parents encourage their children to marry someone of the same race and religion. Still, when young people move away from their parents' home to attend college or to work in another city, they often date and then marry a person from a different ethnic background. Marriages between Americans of different religions or different national origins are common. However, marriages between blacks and whites continue to be rare, involving less than 0.3% of the nation's 58 million married couples.

2. When a man and a woman become engaged, they enter a very exciting and busy period of their lives. At this time, it is traditional for the man to give his fiancée a gift she will wear and treasure for the rest of her life—a diamond **engagement** ring. During the engagement period, the **bride-to-be** and her fiancé meet each other's relatives, if they have not done so already. They also plan their wedding and rent or buy an apartment or house. In the U.S., very few newlyweds begin married life living with either set of parents.

3. Engagement and wedding gifts help the couple to set up their own new home. It is common for engaged couples to go to a department store **bridal registry** and fill out a list of the items they would like to receive. Wedding guests can choose gifts from this list before the wedding and have them mailed to the bride-to-be's home. In addition to wedding gifts, the couple also receives shower gifts. A shower is a party just for women at which each guest gives the bride-to-be something useful for her new home. Also, shortly before the wedding, the **groom** and his close friends and relatives celebrate at an all-male party called a **bachelor** or stag party. On this occasion, the groom often receives gifts, too.

The Big Day

4. Most wedding customs **observed** in the U.S. today began in other countries in the past centuries. Some are based on old **superstitions** about ways to bring the couple good luck and many children. Others **symbolize** the **marital** promise of lifelong **devotion**.

5. The traditional American bride wears a long white **gown** and a veil. In earlier times, people thought the **veil** would protect the bride from evil spirits. The white gown and veil also symbolize **innocence**. Traditional brides also obey the well-known verse and wear "something old, something new, something borrowed, and something blue." The groom usually wears a tuxedo, which is commonly rented just for his wedding day.

6. The wedding ceremony may be held in a church, home, hotel, or nice outdoor area. Guests are seated on either side of the center **aisle**, and the ceremony started with a procession down the aisle. The bridal party includes the bride and groom and their closest relatives and friends. These are usually **bridesmaids** and a maid of honor all wearing matching dresses and the groom's ushers and "best man" (usually his brother or best friend). Walking in front of the bride is a young "flower girl," who throws flower petals from a straw basket. The bride walks down the aisle with her father or both parents, who "give her away" to the groom. The bride and groom then face the cleric or judge **conducting** the service, and a traditional service is recited.

7. During a typical ceremony, the bride and groom exchange **identical** wedding rings. The ring, a circle with no beginning and no end, symbolizes unending love and **loyalty**. It is worn on the fourth finger of the left hand because of a very old (and incorrect) idea that a vein or nerve runs from this finger directly to the heart.

8. At the end of the wedding ceremony, the groom and bride are pronounced husband and wife and are invited to kiss each other. Then, the entire wedding procession walks back up the aisle. After a church wedding, guests may throw rose petals, **confetti**, or rice at the **newlyweds** as they leave the church. Rice, a common **fertility** symbol, is supposed to help the couple have children. Sometimes, the couple's car is decorated with tin cans, paper streamers, or old shoes, along with a "Just Married" sign. The tin cans and shoes reflect an old idea that noisemakers **scare** away evil spirits and bring good luck.

9. After the ceremony, there is a **reception**—a party with food, drinks, and dancing. During the reception, the wedding cake, which is usually tall with white frosting, is **displayed**. Most wedding cakes have a **miniature** bride and groom or miniature wedding bells on top. After the meal, the bride and groom cut the cake and it is served to the guests. Some guests take home a slice of cake in a little box. Some people believe that if a single woman sleeps with this piece of cake under her pillow she will dream of the man she is going to marry. Just before the bride leaves the reception, she throws a **bouquet** of flowers backward over her head to a group of single women standing behind her. Supposedly, the one who catches the bouquet will be the next to marry.

Throwing the bouquet

10. After the wedding, the newlyweds usually take a vacation called a **honeymoon**. This word means "month of honey" in French. It refers to a former custom—for newlyweds to share a drink made with honey everyday during the first month of their marriage.

After You Read

Knowledge Focus

1. Put the following events in chronological order by numbering them 1—7. Start with the earliest.

    ____ wedding day   ____ honeymoon   ____ anniversary
    ____ engagement   ____ shower for the bride-to-be

_____ going out with someone _____ marriage proposal

2. **Understand details.**

   1) Scan Paragraph 6 to look for the people who are part of the wedding party. Name at least 6 people.

   _____ _____ _____ _____ _____ _____

   2) What are the common signs and symbols in an American wedding ceremony? What are the symbolic meanings of the signs and symbols?
   e.g. white gown—purity, innocence

   _____

3. **Mark each statement true (T) or false (F).**

   1) It is common for an American to marry a person from a different ethnic background. _____

   2) Americans usually base their marriage decisions upon practical considerations. _____

   3) The interracial marriages between blacks and whites continue to be rare in the U.S. _____

   4) In the U.S., many parents arrange marriages for their children. _____

   5) It is customary for the bride to wear a wedding veil, which can prevent other people from seeing the bride's face. _____

   6) After the wedding, the bride usually throws the bouquet to the women guests. _____

Language Focus

1. Match the word partners to form collocations. Then use the correct collocations in the following paragraph.

   _____ 1) social   a. consideration
   _____ 2) practical   b. devotion
   _____ 3) department   c. contact
   _____ 4) bridal   d. reception
   _____ 5) lifelong   e. store
   _____ 6) wedding   f. registry

   American people do not like arranged marriages. Before marriage, one first goes out with someone for a while, and usually they know each other through _____. There is not much _____ concerning marriage, and usually American people place priority on "love" over family background or financial conditions. How can the wedding guests know what gifts the couple wants? They can go to the _____ where they can get a list from the _____, and the items on the list are the things the couple wants to receive. On the wedding day, a ceremony is conducted by the minister and there the couple swears their _____ to each other. After the ceremony, there comes the _____ where the wedding guests can enjoy the food, drinks and dances.

2. **Fill in each blank with a suitable preposition or adverb.**
   1) It is traditional for the man to give his fiancée a gift she will wear and treasure _____ the rest of her life.
   2) Engagement and wedding gifts help the couple to set _____ their own new home.
   3) It is common for engaged couples to go to a department store bridal registry and fill _____ a list of the items they would like to receive.
   4) _____ the occasion of a stag party, the groom often receives gifts, too.
   5) The bride walks _____ the aisle with her father or both parents, who "give her _____" to the groom.
   6) The tin cans and shoes reflect an old idea that noisemakers scare _____ evil spirits and bring good luck.

3. **Proofreading and error correction.**
   The passage contains FIVE errors. Each indicated line contains a maximum of ONE error. In each case, only ONE word is involved.

For many, marriage represents the opportunity to express and reinforce a life-long commitment with a loved one. In contemporary America, the marital bond is often characterized by romantic love and emotional intimacy, and many marriages do not conform to this model. For some people, marriage constitutes practical necessity for childrearing and economic survival. In the late twenty and early twenty-first centuries, such developments as blended families, single-parent families, multiple remarriages and new reproductive technologies have challenged rigid conceptions of married life, while often reaffirm the importance of its social and economic support.	1) _____ 2) _____ 3) _____ 4) _____ 5) _____

Comprehensive Work

1. Work in groups of four and share ideas with your team members.

Compare American wedding customs with Chinese wedding customs. Which are the same or similar? Which are different?

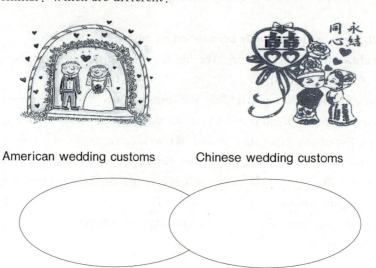

American wedding customs   Chinese wedding customs

2. Essay Writing.

What is likely to happen if a Chinese marry an American?

Text B   Wedding Customs & Superstitions

There are many customs and superstitions associated with weddings. In the past, a wedding was seen as a time when people were particularly susceptible to bad luck and evil spirits. Many originated in or are modifications of customs which began many centuries ago.

Choosing the day

Although most weddings now take place on Saturday, it was considered unlucky in the past. Fridays were also considered unlucky, particularly Friday the 13th. The famous old rhyme advises a wedding day in the first half of the week:

Monday for wealth
Tuesday for health
Wednesday the best day of all
Thursday for losses
Friday for crosses
Saturday for no luck at all

Something old, something new...

Something old, something new
Something borrowed, something blue
And a silver sixpence in your shoe

The rhyme originated in Victorian times although some of the customs referred to in it are much older.

The "something old" represents the couple's friends who will hopefully remain close during the marriage. Traditionally, this was an old garter given to the bride by a happily married woman in the hope that her happiness in marriage would be passed on to the new bride.

The "something new" symbolizes the newlyweds' happy and prosperous future.

The "something borrowed" is often lent by the bride's family and is an item much valued by the family. The bride must return the item to ensure good luck.

The custom of the bride wearing "something blue" originated in ancient Israel where the bride wore a blue ribbon in her hair to represent fidelity.

The placing of a silver sixpence in the bride's shoe was to ensure wealth in the couple's married life. Today some brides substitute a penny in their shoe during the ceremony as silver sixpences are less common.

On the way to the wedding

When the bride is ready to leave the house for the wedding ceremony, a last look in the mirror will bring her good luck. However, returning to the mirror once she has begun her journey will result in bad luck.

Seeing a chimney sweep on the way to a wedding is thought to bring good luck and it is still possible to hire one to attend wedding ceremonies. Other good luck omens seen on the way to the ceremony include lambs, toads, spiders, black cats and rainbows.

Seeing an open grave, a pig, a lizard, or hearing a cockerel crow after dawn are all thought to be omens of bad luck. Monks and nuns are also bad omens. This may be because they are associated with poverty and chastity. They are also thought to signal a dependence on charity by the newlyweds.

Bad weather on the way to the wedding is thought to be an omen of an unhappy marriage, although rain is considered a good omen in some cultures. Cloudy skies and wind are believed to cause stormy marriages. Snow, on the other hand, is associated with fertility and wealth.

Crossing the threshold

After the wedding, the bride must enter the new marital home through the main entrance. It is traditional for the groom to carry the bride over the threshold when they enter for the first time. The reason for this is uncertain. One explanation is that the bride will be visited by bad luck if she falls when entering. An alternative is that the bride will be unlucky if she steps into the new home with the left foot first. The bride can avoid both mishaps by being carried.

Finish the following exercises.

1. Which of the following days is considered lucky for wedding?

    a. Saturday   b. Friday   c. Thursday   d. Wednesday

2. The bride is supposed to wear "something blue," which symbolizes _____.

    a. happiness   b. purity   c. fidelity   d. hope

3. On the way to the wedding, seeing _____ is considered good luck.

    a. a pig, a lizard   b. spiders, black cats   c. monks, nuns

4. Which of the following weather is considered lucky for wedding?

    a. cloudy   b. windy   c. snowy

5. It is traditional for the groom to _____ the bride over the threshold when they enter for the first time.

Unit 9 *Love and Marriage in the U.S.*

Text C   Dating Patterns

In the United States, in general, young people enjoy a great deal of freedom. It is probably also true that American young people have more freedom now than they have ever had before. It is not really clear whether all of this freedom is a good thing with respect to dating relationships. As a result of the freedom that young people have, dating has changed substantially in recent years.

"You said you loved me. I said I loved you... do we mean it? or, are we just running out of things to say?"

In the traditional dating pattern in the United States, much of the responsibility for a date falls on the young man. In this pattern, the young man must first call the girl he wishes to date on the telephone. Usually, this call is made quite early in a week. Most girls in traditional dating relationships expect to get a telephone call from a young man by Wednesday. Most dating occurs on weekends. Many young people do not have to get up early for school or work on Saturday and Sunday mornings, so Friday nights and Saturday nights are popular nights for dates. The young man must ask the girl for the date, and suggest some things that they might do together. It is usually up to the young man to pay for all of the evening's activities.

There are many things to do on dates. Many young people enjoy going to sports events, such as football and baseball games. These games may occur at a high school, college, or in a large sports arena in a city. A very popular place for young people to go on dates is the movies. Almost everyone enjoys a good movie, and almost every town has at least one movie theater. Young people may also enjoy going to a night club or coffee house. Here, they may listen to music and dance, and perhaps meet some of their friends.

In some parts of the United States, traditional dating relationships begin when young people are in high school. In other places, young people do not go out in couples until they are in college, or in their early twenties. Some young men would rather go out with just one girl all of the time. Every Saturday night, a young man will go out with the same girl. Many girls enjoy this kind of relationship also. It gives both the boy and the girl a chance to get to know one another quite well. Sometimes, this may lead to marriage. Other young people enjoy dating different individuals. One week they may go out with one person, the next with another. They get to know many people this way, and may not wish to have a serious relationship with just one person.

Many young people in the United States, especially college students, do not go out on either of these traditional dates. Instead, they go out on group dates. In this kind of dating pattern, small groups of young people go out together. All of the people in the group are usually friends, but some of the people in the group may not know each other. No one young man is with any particular girl. They are all together as part of the group. This is very different from the traditional date.

A group date differs from a traditional date in several ways. First, there are no special relationships in the group. No particular girl and boy are together all the time. Second, the group date may occur on a weekend, but it may not be planned in advance. A group of young people may decide on Saturday afternoon that they want to spend Saturday evening together. They may all decide to go to a movie, or to some other event. On a group date, no one is paired with anyone else.

As a result, every person pays for his or her own expenses. This means that the girls must pay for themselves. They must pay their own admission for the movies, for a cup of coffee, or for anything else that costs money during the date.

Mark each statement with T for true or F for false.
1. On a traditional date, the young man usually calls the girl on Friday nights. _____
2. In most cases, the girl would suggest what to do on the date. _____
3. Some people may not date just one person all the time. _____
4. On a group date, several particular pairs of young men and women go out together. _____
5. Group dates are always very well planned in advance. _____
6. In a group date, every person pays for his or her own expenses. _____

Books to Read

Edith Wharton: *The Age of Innocence*

Society scion Newland Archer is engaged to May Wetland, but his well-ordered life is upset when he meets May's unconventional cousin...

Erich Segal: **Love Story**

He was rich; she was poor. He was sporty; she played music. But they fell in love. This is their story.

Movies to See

Guess Who

A sarcastic father has plenty to say about his daughter wanting to marry a white boy.

My Best Friend's Wedding

Julianne fell in love with her best friend the day he decided to marry someone else.

Sweet Home Alabama

A young woman with a white trash background runs away from her husband in Alabama and reinvents herself as a New York socialite.

Songs to Enjoy

All-4-One: "I Swear"

For better or worse, till death do us part; I'll love you with every beat of my heart...

Diana King: "I Say A Little Prayer"

The moment I wake up, before I put on my makeup, I say a little prayer for you...

Poem to Read

Read the poem. What is the essence of marriage according to the poem?

On Marriage

By Kahlil Gibran

You were born together, and together you shall be forevermore.
You shall be together when white wings of death scatter your days.
Aye, you shall be together even in the silent memory of God.
But let there be spaces in your togetherness,
And let the winds of the heavens dance between you.
Love one another but make not a bond of love:
Let it rather be a moving sea between the shores of your souls.
Fill each other's cup but drink not from one cup.
Give one another of your bread but eat not from the same loaf.
Sing and dance together and be joyous, but let each one of you be alone,

Even as the strings of a lute are alone though they quiver with the same music.
Give your hearts, but not into each other's keeping.
For only the hand of Life can contain your hearts.
And stand together, yet not too near together:
For the pillars of the temple stand apart,
And the oak tree and the cypress grow not in each other's shadow.

Unit 10
Family Life in the U. S.

> The Americans has fashioned anew the features of his family institutions, as he does everything else about him.
> —Max Lerner

Unit Goals

- To get a general knowledge of the American family
- To learn some basic values concerning the American family
- To get acquainted with some American etiquette
- To develop critical thinking and intercultural communication skills
- To learn useful words and expressions concerning American family life and etiquette and improve English language skills

Before You Read

1. Here are some American proverbs and sayings. Can you find similar sayings in Chinese?
   1) As the twig is bent, so grows the tree.
   2) The child is a chip off the old block.
   3) A man may work from sun to sun, but a woman's work is never done.
   4) Behind every successful man, there's a woman.
   5) Blood is thicker than water.
   6) An old man is treasure of a family.

2. Interview your partner on the following questions.
   1) What type of family do you live in?
   2) What other family types do you know?
   3) What is the parent-child relationship like in your family?
   4) What kind of parent-child relationship do you expect?

5) What do you usually do for your family?

Start to Read

Text A American Family

Family Structures

1. What is the typical American family like? If Americans are asked to name the members of the families, family **structure** becomes clear. Married American adults will name their husband or wife and their children, if they have any, as their **immediate** family. If they mention their father, mother, sisters, or brothers, they will define them as separate units, usually living in separate households. Aunts, uncles, cousins and grandparents are considered **extended** family.

2. Traditionally, the American family has been a nuclear family, **consisting** of a husband, wife and their children, living in a house or apartment. Grandparents rarely live in the same home with their married sons and daughters, and uncles and aunts almost never do. In the 1950s, the majority of the American households were the **classic** traditional American family—a husband, wife, and two children. The father was the "**breadwinner**"; the mother was the "**homemaker**" and they have two children under the age of eighteen. If you said the word *family* to Americans a generation ago, this was the traditional picture that probably came into their minds.

3. Today, however, the reality is much different. A very small percentage of American households consist of a working father, a stay-at-home mother, and children under eighteen. Only about one quarter of American households now consist of two parents and their children, and the majority of these mothers hold jobs outside the home. The majority of American households today consist of married couples without children, single parents and their children, or unrelated people living together. Perhaps most surprising, 25 percent of Americans live alone.

4. What has happened to the traditional American family of the 1950s, and why? In the 1950s, men who had fought in World War II had returned home, married, and started their families. There was a **substantial** increase in the birthrate, producing the "baby **boomers**." However, today young people are marrying and having children later in life. And some couples now even choose not to have children at all. Besides, the people are living longer after their children are grown, and they often end up alone. Another factor that helps produce the changes in the traditional family structure is the high rate of divorce.

The Children and the Elderly Parents

5. American children have been expected to "leave the nest" at about age eighteen, after they graduate from high school. At that time they are expected to go on to college (many go to another city) or to get a job and support themselves. By their mid-twenties, if children are still living with their parents, some people will suspect that something is wrong. Traditionally, children have been given a lot of freedom and equality in the family so that they will grow up to be independent, self-reliant adults. Today,

"I THINK IT'S ABOUT TIME HE LEFT HOME."

however, a number of young people are unable to find jobs that support the lifestyle they have grown up with, and they choose to move back in with their parents for a time. These young people are sometimes called "**boomerang** kids," because they have left the nest once but are now back again.

6. Although adult children sometimes come home to Mom and Dad, middle-aged and elderly people try to avoid moving in with their grown children. Older people take pride in their independence, enjoy their freedom, and do not want to be a burden to their children. The telephone, the car, the airplane, and e-mail keep families in close contact even when they live in different parts of the country.

7. Sometimes, newcomers to the U.S. **mistakenly** conclude that Americans simply leave their elderly parents in nursing homes and forget about them. Actually, only about 5% of today's **senior** citizens live in nursing homes. Millions of middle-aged Americans—members of the "sandwich generation"— take care of both their elderly parents and their children. However, for elderly

people who are very ill or **disabled**, a nursing home may be the only **alternative** if their children are working and no one is home during the day to take care of them. Family members usually select a nursing home nearby so that they can visit often. Americans are constantly seeking new ways of caring for increasing numbers of older people with physical limitations.

Where Is Home?

8. The majority of Americans live in or near large cities, but small-town living is still **widespread**. A suburb **combines** the advantages of safer, more **intimate** small-town life with the **recreational** and cultural facilities and job opportunities of the big city nearby. About two-thirds of Americans live in homes or apartments that they own, but many people rent their residences.

9. For the typical American family, home may be in a different place every five or six years. Every year, about 16% of Americans change residences. All this moving **deprives** the nuclear family of having many relatives and longtime friends living nearby. But family members hop into a car or onto a plane to come together for major turning points in one another's lives. Such events include birthdays, graduations, weddings, anniversaries, and funerals. Family parties may be all the more joyous when they bring together relatives who have not seen each other for a while.

After You Read

Knowledge Focus

1. **Consider the following questions.**
   1) What has caused the changes in American family structure?
   2) Why do you think that many elderly people in the U.S. choose to live apart from their grown children?
   3) Why do you think that most Americans move a lot in their life time?
   4) Where do you prefer to live, the city or the countryside? Why?
   5) Which would be your choice, to rent a house or to buy a house? Why?

2. What are the meanings of the following expressions?
   1) "breadwinner" _____
   2) "baby boomers" _____
   3) "boomerang kids" _____
   4) "homemaker" _____
   5) "leave the nest" _____
   6) "sandwich generation" _____

3. Mark each statement with T if it is true or F if it is false.
   1) Traditionally, the American family has been a nuclear family. _____
   2) Most American households now consist of two parents and their children. _____
   3) The high rate of divorce helps produce the changes in the traditional family structure. _____
   4) American children have been expected to "leave the nest" after they graduate from college. _____
   5) Most of today's senior citizens live in nursing homes. _____
   6) About two-thirds of Americans live in homes or apartments that they own. _____

Language Focus

1. Complete the following sentences with the proper words and expressions.

household	come into one's mind	consist of
substantial	alternative end up	take pride in
combine...with...	deprive...of...	all the more

   1) A good idea has just _____. Come here and listen to me.
   2) The spread of television has considerably _____ us _____ our time for reading.
   3) She was irritated by his lateness, and his excuse made her _____ angry.
   4) The product is so successful that its name has become a _____ word.
   5) As Chinese, we all _____ the remarkable success of our country.
   6) Shall we have a light meal or a _____ one?
   7) How many players does a baseball team _____?
   8) It's an essential principle that we must _____ theory _____ practice.
   9) I had no _____ but to accept the offer.
   10) If you continue to steal, you will _____ in prison.

2. Fill in each blank with a suitable preposition or adverb.
   1) Traditionally, the American family has been a nuclear family, consisting _____ a husband, wife and their children, living in a house or apartment.
   2) The father was the "breadwinner," the mother was the "homemaker," and they have two children _____ the age of eighteen.
   3) There was a substantial increase _____ the birthrate, producing the "baby

boomers."

4) The people are living longer after their children are grown, and they often end _____ alone.

5) The telephone, the car, the airplane, and e-mail keep families _____ close contact even when they live in different parts of the country.

6) Americans are constantly seeking new ways of caring _____ increasing numbers of older people _____ physical limitations.

3. **Proofreading and error correction.**

The passage contains FIVE errors. Each indicated line contains a maximum of ONE error. In each case, only ONE word is involved.

The U.S. Census statistics indicate changes in family structure over time. Since 1970, delays in marriage and increase in divorce rates have contributed to reduce the number of people living in family households. Divorce is common, with 50 percent of all marriages end in divorce. The number of single women raising children have doubled. "Blended" families due to remarriage create complex step-parenting relationships. Women are also joining the workforce at unprecedented rate.	1) _____ 2) _____ 3) _____ 4) _____ 5) _____

Comprehensive Work

1. **Share ideas with your team members.**

   Work in groups. Discuss the differences between Chinese and American families in child-rearing.

   1) Who makes the important decisions in the family?
      American Family: _____
      Chinese Family: _____
   2) Do unmarried children leave home and live independently?
      American Family: _____
      Chinese Family: _____
   3) Are children expected to work during their school years?
      American Family: _____
      Chinese Family: _____
   4) What is considered to be the true expression of real family feeling?
      American Family: _____
      Chinese Family: _____

2. **Essay Writing.**

Do you agree that unhappy couples should stay married just for the sake of their children? Why or why not?

Read More

Text B　　Divorce

 Americans believe that they are entitled to happiness, and they expect marriage to contribute to their enjoyment of life. If the couple is not happy, the individuals may choose to get a divorce. For every 100 marriages that take place today in America, there are about 50 divorces. The U.S. divorce rate is twice that of Europe and three times higher than Japan's.

What goes wrong? The fact that divorce is so common in the U.S. does not mean that Americans consider marriage a casual, unimportant relationship. Just the opposite is true. Americans expect a great deal from marriage. They prefer no marriage at all to a marriage without love and understanding.

The majority of adult Americans believe that unhappy couples should not stay married just because they have children at home, a significant change in attitude since the 1950s. Many people do not believe in sacrificing individual happiness for the sake of the children. They say that children may be better off living with one parent than with two who are constantly arguing. Divorce now is so common that it is no longer socially unacceptable, and children are not embarrassed to say that their parents are divorced. A divorce is relatively easy to obtain in most parts of the United States. Most states have "no fault" divorce. To obtain a no-fault divorce, a couple states that they can no longer live happily together and they have irreconcilable differences. That is neither partner's fault.

If a divorcing couple has children, the court must determine which parent the children will live with and who will provide for their support. In most cases, the children live with the mother and the father pays child support and has visitation rights. However, it is not uncommon for a father to get full custody

or joint custody when this arrangement is in the children's best interests.

The high risk of divorce does not seem to make Americans afraid to marry again. Remarriage and the creation of new, blended families are extremely common in the U.S. One American joke tells of a wife calling to her second husband, "Quick, John! Come here and help me! Your children and my children are beating up our children!"

Answer the following questions.
1. Why is divorce rate very high in America?
2. What is a non-fault divorce?
3. What would become of the children of the divorced couple?

Text C Decay of Family Relationships

By Allan Bloom

The decay of the natural ground for the family relationships was largely unanticipated and unprepared for in the early modern thinkers. But they did suggest a certain reform of the family, reflecting the movement away from the constraints of duty, toward reliance on those elements of the family that could be understood to flow out of free expressions of personal sentiment. In Locke, paternal authority is turned into parental authority, a rejection of a father's divine or natural right to rule and to rule permanently, in favor of a father's and a mother's right to care for their children as long as they need care, for the sake of the children's freedom—which the child will immediately recognize, when he reaches majority, to have been for his own benefit. There is nothing left of the reverence toward the father as the symbol of the divine on earth, the unquestioned bearer of authority. Rather, sons and daughters will calculate that they have benefited from their parents' care, which prepared them for the freedom they enjoy, and they will be grateful, although they have no reciprocal duty, except insofar as they wish to leave behind a plausible model for the conduct of their own children toward them. They may, if they please, obey their father in order to inherit his estate, if he has one, which he can dispose of as he pleases. From the point of view of the children, the family retains its validity on the basis of modern principles, and Locke prepares the way for the democratic family, so movingly described by Tocqueville in *Democracy in America*.

So far, so good. The children are reconciled to the family. But the problem, it seems to me, is in the motive of the parents to care for their children. The children can say to their parents: "You are strong, and we are weak. Use your strength to help us. You are rich, and we are poor. Spend your money on us. You are wise, and we are ignorant. Teach us." But why should mother and father want to do so much, involving so much sacrifice without any reward? Perhaps parental care is a duty, or family life has great joys. But neither of these is a conclusive reason when rights and individual autonomy hold sway. The children have unconditional need for and receive unquestionable benefits from the parents; the same cannot be asserted about parents.

Locke believed, and the events of our time seem to confirm his belief, that women have an instinctive attachment to children that cannot be explained as self-interest or calculation. The attachment of mother and child is perhaps the only undeniable natural social bond. It is not always effective, and it can, with effort, be suppressed, but it is always a force. And this is what we see today. But what about the father? Maybe he loves imagining his own eternity through the generations stemming from him. But this is only an act of imagination, one that can be attenuated by other concerns and calculations, as well as by his losing faith in the continuation of his name for very long in the shifting conditions of democracy. Of necessity, therefore, it was understood to be the woman's job to get and hold the man by her charms and wiles because, by nature, nothing else would induce him to give up his freedom in favor of the heavy duties of family. But women no longer wish to do this, and they, with justice, consider it unfair according to the principles governing us. So the cement that bound the family together crumbled. It is not the children who break away; it is the parents who abandon them. Women are no longer willing to make unconditional and perpetual commitments on unequal terms, and, no matter what they hope, nothing can effectively make most men share equally the responsibilities of childbearing and childrearing. The divorce rate is only the most striking symptom of this breakdown.

None of this results from the sixties, or from the appeal to masculine vanity begun by advertisers in the fifties, or from any other superficial, pop-culture events. More than two hundred years ago Rousseau saw with alarm the seeds of the breakdown of the family in liberal society, and he dedicated much of his genius to trying to correct it. He found that the critical connection between man and woman was being broken by individualism, and focused his efforts, theoretical and practical, on encouraging passionate romantic love in them. He wanted to rebuild and reinforce that connection, previously encumbered by now discredited religious and civil regulation, on modern grounds of desire and consent. He retraced the picture of nature that had become a palimpsest under the abrasion of modern criticism, and he enticed men and women into admiring its teleological ordering, specifically the complementarity between the two sexes, which mesh and set the machine of life in motion, each differing from and needing the other, from the depths of the body to the heights of the soul. He set utter abandon to the sentiments and imaginations of idealized love against calculation of individual interest. Rousseau inspired a whole genre of novelistic and poetic literature that lived feverishly for over a century, coexisting with the writings of the Benthams and the Mills who were earnestly at work homogenizing the sexes. His undertaking had the heaviest significance because human community was at risk. In essence he was persuading women freely to be different from men and to take on the burden of entering a positive contract with the family, as opposed to a negative, individual, self-protective contract with the state. Tocqueville picked up this theme and described the absolute differentiation of husband's and wife's functions and ways of life in the American family. This he contrasted to the disorder, nay, chaos, of Europe, which he attributed to a misunderstanding or misapplication of the principle of equality—only an abstraction when not informed by nature's imperatives.

Finish the exercises.
Agree or Disagree? Share ideas with your partner on the following points.
1. In family relations, parental authority should take the place of paternal authority.
2. Leaving no reverence toward the father as the unquestioned bearer of authority is a right thing.
3. The children have unconditional need for and receive unquestionable benefits from the parents.
4. The attachment of mother and child is perhaps the only undeniable natural social bond.
5. To get married and become a parent means to give up his/her freedom in favor of the heavy duties of family.
6. The critical connection between man and woman is being broken by individualism.

7. Women should be different from men and take on the burden of entering a positive contract with the family, as opposed to a negative, individual, self-protective contract with the state.

For Fun

Books to Read

Maxine Hong Kingston: *The Woman Warrior*

A Chinese woman explains how her identity was formed growing up in California and learning about her culture through family stories and Chinese myths.

Henrik Ibsen: *A Doll's House*

Nora realized the need for a new-found freedom for women amid a suffocating society governed wholly by unsympathetic and insensitive men.

Movies and TV Series to See

Kramer vs. Kramer

A just divorced man must learn to care for his son on his own, and then must fight in court to keep custody of him.

 Modern Family

Three different, but related families face trials and tribulations in their own uniquely comedic ways.

Family Man

A fast-lane investment broker, offered the opportunity to see how the other half lives, wakes up to find that his sports car and girlfriend have become a mini-van and wife.

Song to Enjoy

Jackie Deshannon: "What the World Needs Now Is Love"

What the world needs now is love, sweet love; No, not just for some, but for everyone ...

Poem to Read

Read the poem and try to translate it into Chinese.

On Children

By Kahlil Gibran

Your children are not your children.

They are the sons and daughters of Life's longing for itself.

They come through you but not from you,

And though they are with you, yet they belong not to you.

You may give them your love but not your thoughts.

For they have their own thoughts.

You may house their bodies but not their souls,

For their souls dwell in the house of tomorrow, which you cannot visit, not even in your dreams.

You may strive to be like them, but seek not to make them like you.

For life goes not backward nor tarries with yesterday.

You are the bows from which your children as living arrows are sent forth.

The archer sees the mark upon the path of the infinite, and He bends you with His might that His arrows may go swift and far.

Let your bending in the archer's hand be for gladness;

For even as He loves the arrow that flies, so He loves also the bow that is stable.

Unit 11
Holidays and Festivals in the U.S.

Ring out the old, ring in the new,
Ring happy bells across the snow;
The year is going, let him go;
Ring out the false, ring in the true.
　　　　　　　—Alfred, Lord Tennyson

Unit Goals

- To get a general knowledge of the American festivals
- To learn how Americans observe their festivals
- To develop critical thinking and intercultural communication skills
- To learn useful words and expressions concerning American holidays and festivals and improve English language skills

Before You Read

Test your knowledge on American festivals.

Different festivals are connected with different symbols. Try the quiz exercises and see how much you know about the American holidays.

① ② ③

④ ⑤ ⑥

Mother's Day	_____	Easter	_____
Halloween	_____	Valentine's Day	_____
Thanksgiving Day	_____	Christmas	_____

Start to Read

Text A The Winter Holiday Season

Merry Christmas!

1. Santa Claus, snowmen, bright lights, colorful **decorations**, bells, and traditional songs—all these help to make December the most **festive** month of the year. As the month **progresses** toward the winter solstice, the daylight hours grow shorter and shorter. In the northern part of the U.S., winter weather can be "frightful." Yet even winter snowstorms cannot bury that **contagious** feeling of festivity.

2. Why does almost everybody feel so good? It is gift-giving time, party time, and vacation time. Students from elementary school through college have about 2 weeks' vacation, beginning shortly before Christmas and ending soon after New Year's Day. Many families go away for the holidays to visit relatives in another state, ski in the mountains, or sunbathe on the beaches in the South. But those who stay home have fun, too. Parities **abound** to celebrate Christmas and the arrival of the New Year. Even the workplace is festive, thanks to the traditions of office parties and holiday **bonuses**.

3. Since 86% of Americans are **Christian**, December 25 is both a religious and

a legal holiday. Most businesses are closed on Christmas Day. Many families go to church on Christmas Eve or Christmas morning. After services, they gather around the tree and open their gifts. Then they enjoy a traditional Christmas dinner—turkey or ham, sweet potatoes, vegetables, and cranberry sauce. Dessert is usually fruit cake, plum pudding, or mince pie.

4. Most of the Christmas customs that Americans enjoy today are **variations** of traditions brought to America by European immigrants. Some go back to ancient times.

5. *Exchanging Gifts*. In the U.S., it is **customary** to exchange gifts with family members and close friends. Both children and adults get Christmas presents, although children usually get many more.

6. *Receiving Toys from Santa Claus*. Many American children believe that on Christmas Eve, Santa Claus **slides** down their chimney to bring them gifts. According to the story, Santa Claus flies through the air in a **sleigh** pulled by eight **reindeer**. Several days or weeks before Christmas, children tell Santa what toys they want by writing him letters or visiting him in a  local department store. As in Great Britain, American children hang **stockings** hoping that Santa will fill them with candy and toys. Traditionally, stockings were hung near the **fireplace**, but today children hang them wherever they think Santa will see them!

7. *Decorating the Home with Holiday Plants*. The winter custom of decorating homes and churches with evergreens began in ancient times. Branches of fir or spruce were thought to bring good luck and **guarantee** the return of spring. The early Germans believed that in winter, evil spirits killed plants and trees  and caused green leaves and flowers to disappear. Bringing evergreens into their homes was supposed to protect them from death. In ancient times, **mistletoe** was hung over doorways for good luck. Today the custom continues, but now it is for fun. Anyone standing under the mistletoe is supposed to get kissed.

8. *Going Caroling*. In the early days of the Christian Church, the bishops sang **carols** on Christmas Day. Now, soloists and choirs on the radio, on TV,

in church, and in school all help fill the winter with beautiful music. Copying an old English custom, many Americans go caroling—walking with friends from house to house singing the traditional holiday songs.

9. *Sending Christmas Cards*. The custom of sending Christmas cards began in London in 1843 and came to the U.S. in 1875. Today, most Americans send dozens of season's greeting cards to relatives, friends, and business associates.

Happy New Year!

10. The country's most crowded New Year's Eve celebration takes place in New York City's Times Square. Since 1907, the famous ball-lowering ceremony has been a holiday **highlight**. To celebrate the arrival of the year 2000, an **estimated** 2 million people crowded into Times Square, and hundreds of millions viewed the scene on TV. The huge, 1,070-pound lighted crystal ball began its **descent** from a 77-foot **flagpole** at 11:59 p.m. and reached the bottom at exactly midnight. **Simultaneously**, confetti, balloons, and fireworks brightened the night sky. It was the biggest public event ever held in the city.

11. The New Year arrives earlier in the East than in other parts of the country. When midnight comes to New York, it is 11 p.m. in Chicago, 10 p.m. in Denver, and only 9 p.m. in Los Angeles. The **contiguous** 48 states span four time zones; Alaska and Hawaii add two more.

12. What do Americans do on New Year's Day? Many sleep late because they stayed up all night long. Many watch TV, which offers **spectacular parades** and football games between champion college teams. From ancient times to present, New Year's customs have been connected with saying goodbye to the past and looking forward to a better future. Therefore, New Year's Day often **inspires** people to start new programs and give up bad habits. Some people make New Year's **resolutions**, promises to themselves to improve their behavior. People talk about "turning over a new

leaf," referring to a clean, blank page or a fresh start. Typical New Year's resolutions are to spend less money, give up smoking, begin a diet, or be nicer to others. It is safe to **assume** about half of them are forgotten by January 31!

13. Some people prefer to see the old year out at a church service. Although the holiday does not have religious origin, many churches hold "Watch Night" services on New Year's Eve.

14. The custom of visiting friends, relatives and neighbors is one of the popular activities on New Year's Day. This activity is called Open House. The custom was **inaugurated** by George Washington during his first term as president. On January 1, 1789, President Washington first opened the doors of his official residence to all who wished to come. An Open House is just what the name implies: the front door is left open, and guests are free to arrive and leave when they like. Invitations may say simply, "Drop in after the game" or "Come drink a New Year's toast with us." On January 1, families hold "Open House," so that their friends can visit them throughout the day to express good wishes for the New Year.

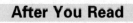

After You Read

Knowledge Focus

1. **Consider the following questions.**
   1) Why is December the most festive month of the year?
   2) How do Americans celebrate Christmas?
   3) How do American people celebrate New Year?
   4) What New Year's resolution will you make this year?

2. **Understand details.**

   Put a tick (√) in the column if the custom is associated with that holiday. Some customs may be traditional on both holidays.

Customs	Christmas	New Year
Exchanging gift around a tree		
Kissing under the mistletoe		
Promising to improve oneself		
Going caroling		

(continued)

Customs	Christmas	New Year
Attending church services		
Watching the ball-drop		
Talking or writing to Santa Claus		
Sending season's greeting cards		
Watch the Bowl games on TV		

Language Focus

1. **Complete the following sentences with the proper words and expressions.**

festive	contiguous	progress (v.)	contagious
thanks to	abound	bonus	descent
customary	guarantee	estimate	highlight
be supposed to	assume	slide	

   1) Scarlet fever is highly _____. Please stay away from the patient.
   2) You _____ tip the waiter when eating out in an American restaurant.
   3) Her performance was the _____ of the show.
   4) The police _____ the number of demonstrators at about 5,000.
   5) During the Spring Festival, the whole country is bathed in a _____ atmosphere.
   6) I _____ that I will pay off my debt by the end of the year.
   7) The spectators watched the _____ of the balloon.
   8) She _____ into the room, not wanting to wake the baby.
   9) England is _____ with Wales.
   10) It was _____ his advice that I succeeded at last.
   11) It is _____ to give people gifts on their birthdays.
   12) Products _____ in this area and people here live in plenty.
   13) Don't worry. The work is _____ steadily.
   14) He's not such a fool as you _____ him to be.
   15) He often overworks, and that's the reason he gets more _____.

2. **Fill in each blank with a suitable preposition or adverb.**

   1) As the month progresses _____ the winter solstice, the daylight hours grow shorter and shorter.
   2) Even the workplace is festive, thanks _____ the traditions of office parties and holiday bonuses.
   3) Most businesses are closed _____ Christmas Day.
   4) Santa Claus flies _____ the air in a sleigh pulled by eight reindeer.
   5) American children hang stockings hoping that Santa will fill them _____ candy and toys.

6) On New Year's Day, many Americans sleep late because they stayed _____ all night long.
7) From ancient times to present, New Year's customs have been connected with saying goodbye to the past and looking forward _____ a better future.
8) Some people prefer to see the old year _____ at a church service.

3. **Proofreading and error correction.**

   The passage contains FIVE errors. Each indicated line contains a maximum of ONE error. In each case, only ONE word is involved.

Holidays are embody multiple calendars, memories and agendas within contemporary American society. Many formal national holidays tend to reinforce shared civic and historical values, yet they also have become foci of protest, which illustrated in the anti-Vietnam War book and movie *Born on the Fourth of July*. Other celebrations are divided by religion, ethnicity region and political meanings. Moreover, holidays vary on scope and seriousness. Thanksgiving produces national respite (and the heaviest travel of the year as families re-unite), when President's Day (combining Washington's and Lincoln's birthdays) is generally marked only by department-store sales, school lessons and post office closings.	1) _____ 2) _____ 3) _____ 4) _____ 5) _____

Comprehensive Work

1. **Share ideas with your team members.**

   Nowadays, many Chinese people begin to observe western festivals like Christmas, Valentine's Day, etc. What do you think of the phenomenon? Should Chinese people observe western festivals or not?

   Divide into two teams and have a debate.
   1) Chinese people should observe western festivals.
      Firstly, _____
      Secondly, _____
      ...
   2) Chinese people should NOT observe western festivals.
      Firstly, _____
      Secondly, _____
      ...

2. **Essay Writing.**

Should a nation attach great significance to its own traditional festivals? Why or why not?

Read More

Text B　　American Vacations

Since the 1940s, almost every American employee has received an annual vacation with pay, and it has become customary to use this time off for travel. Vacations are usually family affairs. Some families stay home to enjoy the local recreational facilities. But most vacationers prefer to travel, either within the United States or to other countries.

The nation's major cities are among its most popular tourist attractions. All year round, tourists jam the streets and hotels of Manhattan; they come to see the skyscrapers, visit museums, art galleries, theaters, and famous specialty shops, and eat in the elegant and exotic restaurants. Besides New York, people are also attracted by cities like Los Angeles, San Francisco, New Orleans, and Philadelphia. With Hollywood as the home of the American movie industry, and Disneyland, the nation's most fabulous amusement park, Los Angeles becomes a fascinating place for people of all ages. As for San Francisco, it is the leading seaport of the Pacific Coast. It is famous for its bridges, cable cars, breathtaking scenery and seafood. To the visitors, New Orleans has its especial attraction. With many remainders of Old Europe and the Old south, this birthplace of jazz gives people a feeling of continental flavor. Compared with other cities, Philadelphia stands as a historical place. People come here to see the Liberty Bell that had announced the signing of the *Declaration of Independence*, and visit the building where the nation's Constitution had been signed.

American cities do offer much for tourists to see. But more people prefer to vacation in a rustic setting. For these people particularly, an automobile gives them great convenience.

Camping has become extremely popular in recent years. They can find a campsite in a quiet valley in the Rockies. They hire horses, ride and hike alongside the river, deep into the mountains. The Americans love this sort of outdoor life in wilderness, in which there is a touch of challenge.

In many parts of the country, cottages are rented during the summer months. City families find the cottage near the ocean or in the woods a refreshing change from urban life. Frequently, mother and the children stay at the cottage all summer, and dad drives up to spend weekends with the family.

Summer vacations have become traditional because most children are not in school during July and August. However, many families take short winter vacations too—especially during the Christmas Season. Skiing, skating, and various kinds of sledding are available in almost all the northern states during the winter months.

Nevertheless, most Americans have a desire to visit other countries. And they are free to go almost anywhere in the world. Obtaining passport is a routine matter. So, millions of Americans travel to Canada and Mexico every year. The islands of the Caribbean are also big tourist attractions. And about 3 million Americans visit Europe every year.

Whether one chooses to travel within the U.S. or abroad, for most Americans a vacation stands as an attractive opportunity for fun, relaxation, and a change of scene. It's a chance for family members to spend leisure time together and get to know each other better. It is one of the happiest of American traditions.

Finish the following exercises.

1. Matching: What are the places famous for?

New York	amusement park
Hollywood	birthplace of jazz
Disneyland	Liberty Bell
San Francisco	skyscrapers
New Orleans	bridges & seafood
Philadelphia	movie industry

2. American cities do offer much for tourists to see. But more people prefer to vacation in a rustic setting. Which of the following scenes is related to the "rustic" setting?
   a. skyscrapers   b. cottages   c. museums

3. Many families take short winter vacations in almost all the northern states during the winter months. Sports like _____, _____, and _____ are among the popular ones.

4. Most Americans have a desire to visit other countries, but the passport is very hard to get. The statement is _____. (true / false)

Text C American Holidays

January 1 is New Year's Day. The night before is called New Year's Eve. On this night, people gather for parties as they wait for the New Year to begin after 12 p.m. On New Year's Day, families enjoy watching university football games to find the national champion. Martin Luther King Day is on the 3rd Monday in January. This famous black American gave the speech, "I Have a Dream." This speech is important for it is about all races in America to enjoy equality.

February 14 is Valentine's Day. A valentine is a very colorful card given to a lover. Gifts are given to the person they love, often flowers for women and a tie or book for a man. February 12 (Abraham Lincoln's birthday) and February 22 (George Washington's birthday) are celebrated together on the Monday between these two days. It is called President's Day.

March 17 is Saint Patrick's Day. Patrick was the Italian priest who brought Christian teachings to Ireland and Europe. On this day, school students must wear green, the color of Ireland. If they do not, they can be pinched by their classmates. At the end of March, schools give students a one-week holiday called Spring Vacation.

April is the month of the Jewish Passover when the Jewish people escaped from Egypt where they were held as slaves. Easter is on the first Sunday after the first full moon following the vernal equinox. The holiday has many traditions. It celebrates the end of Jesus's life called the Resurrection. Children color boiled eggs brought by the Easter bunny. Women wear a new colorful dress or an Easter hat. On the fourth Wednesday, there is Secretaries Day when workers bring flowers or candy to secretaries.

May is known for Mother's Day on the second Sunday. It is the best day for restaurants in America as mothers are guests for a dinner paid for by the father or married children. The last holiday is Memorial Day when families go to cemeteries to honor ancestors.

June is known for Father's Day on the third Sunday. This time the father is the honored person for the day.

July has the most important political holiday called Independence Day. It is always on July 4 and Americans remember the same day in 1776 when America won the war against Great Britain. The *Declaration of Independence* written by Thomas Jefferson was an important paper at this time. Chinese firecrackers and colorful rockets are important in this celebration every year.

August has no important holidays. Parents spend much money on school clothes, so children are interested in shopping at this time. Pencils, pens, notebooks, backpacks, and a colorful lunch box are necessary for all children.

September honors all workers on Labor Day on the first Monday. The weather is very good everywhere, so many businesses invite their workers to have a picnic at a park. The children play many games together. The parents bring a lunch of fried chicken, brown beans, potatoes, fruit (apples, oranges or bananas), drink (milk, fruit juice, or a soft drink) and cookies, pies, or cakes. It is a wonderful family time each year.

October 31 is Halloween. This holiday is for children to dress in costumes that look very scary. They often dress as witches, ghosts, or other characters. Some wear masks of important people like movie stars or presidents. They go to each house and ask for candy by saying "Trick or Treat." Every family gives candy as a treat, but if they do not, the children might do a trick like putting soap on window or letting air out of a tire.

November has Veteran's Day on November 11 to honor soldiers. The fourth Thursday is Thanksgiving, a time to remember the first Americans who survived a hard winter. Local Indians brought them food and they gave thanks to God for the harvest season. Now families give thanks to God for many things.

December has Christmas on December 25. This is the best family holiday, similar to the Spring Festival in China. It remembers the birth of Jesus Christ. Many gifts are given to each family member. The music of this season is the best of the year. All the houses are decorated inside and outside with beautiful colored lights. A Christmas tree is the center of attention in the living room.

Arrange the following American festivals in chronological order.

① Thanksgiving Day　　② Fool's Day　　③ Christmas Day
④ Father's Day　　　　⑤ Independence Day
⑥ Veterans' Day　　　　⑦ Labor Day　　　　⑧ Halloween
⑨ St. Valentine's Day　⑩ New Year's Day

_____ (January 1)

_____ (February 14)

_____ (April 1)

_____ (Third Sunday in June)
_____ (July 4)
_____ (First Monday in September)
_____ (October 31)
_____ (November 11)
_____ (Fourth Thursday in November)
_____ (December 25)

Proper Names

Chicago	n.	芝加哥(美国伊利诺伊州一大城市)
Denver	n.	丹佛(美国科罗拉多州首府)
Los Angeles	n.	洛杉矶(美国加利福尼亚州城市)
Alaska	n.	阿拉斯加(美国州名)
Manhattan	n.	曼哈顿(美国纽约市中心);曼哈顿商业区
New Orleans	n.	新奥尔良(美国路易斯安那州港口城市)
Philadelphia	n.	费城(美国宾夕法尼亚州东南部港市)
Rockies	n.	落基山脉(位于美国西北部)
Caribbean	n.	加勒比海地区(的)

Notes

1. **Alfred, Lord Tennyson** (1809—1892) was Poet Laureate of the United Kingdom and remains one of the most popular English poets. One of Tennyson's most famous works is *Idylls of the King* (1885), a series of narrative poems based on King Arthur and the Arthurian tales.

2. **Martin Luther King, Jr.** (1929—1968) was an American reverend, activist and prominent leader in the American civil rights movement. In 1964, King became the youngest person to receive the Nobel Peace Prize for his work to end segregation and racial discrimination through civil disobedience and other non-violent means. King was assassinated on April 4, 1968, in Memphis, Tennessee. Martin Luther King Day was established as a national holiday in the United States in 1986.

For Fun

Movies to See

Bad Santa

A miserable conman and his partner pose as Santa, and they run into problems when the conman befriends a troubled kid...

Serendipity

Jonathan and Sara met while shopping for gloves in New York and a night of Christmas shopping turned into romance.

Groundhog Day

A weatherman finds himself living the same day over and over again.

Songs to Enjoy

Sarah Connor: "Christmas in My Heart"

Everywhere I go and everyone I know is making lots of wishes for old Santa Claus...

Dolly Parton: "Jingle Bells"

Jingle bells, jingle bells, jingle all the way. Oh, what fun it is to ride, in a one-horse open sleigh...

Unit 12
Sports in the U. S.

> The winners in life think constantly in terms of I can, I will, and I am. Losers, on the other hand, concentrate their waking thoughts on what they should have or would have done, or what they can't do.
>
> —Denis Waitley

Unit Goals

- To get a general view of American sports
- To understand Americans' attitude towards sports
- To recognize the relationship between sports and some American values
- To develop critical thinking and intercultural communication skills
- To learn useful words and expressions concerning American sports and improve English language skills

 Before You Read

Consider the following questions.
1. What is your favorite sport? What can you gain by taking the sport?
2. What are the advantages and disadvantages of playing competitive sports?
3. What activity would you perform to accomplish each goal? Write one activity on each line.
    1) become physically fit: _____
    2) learn something new: _____
    3) do something creative: _____
    4) have a great adventure: _____
    5) learn to be a good team-player: _____

Start to Read

Text A Sports in the U.S.

The Big Three Team Sports

1. Team sports appeal to Americans' love of socializing and competing. The most popular team sports in the U.S.—baseball, football, and basketball—are both **spectator** sports and **participatory** sports. Boys and girls begin playing softball (a game similar to baseball but with a bigger, softer ball) when they are about 9 or 10 years old. In high school and college, football and baseball are played primarily by boys and men, and basketball is played by both sexes.

2. Baseball is often called the national **pastime**. People from other countries sometimes wonder why Americans enjoy this sport so much. "It's dull," they say. "Most of the time, the players are just standing still, waiting for someone to hit the ball." And that's true. But hitting that ball is quite a **challenge**. A **pitch** thrown by a **professional pitcher** usually travels more than 90 miles (145 kilometers) an hour. Hitting a ball thrown that fast is a difficult challenge for any **athlete**, so when a **batter** hits the ball out of the ball park (a home run!), the fans scream and cheer. The professional baseball season ends with the World Series, seven games played between the nation's top two teams. As with **championship** football, fans sometimes pay hundreds of dollars for a ticket to a World Series game. But those that watch the games at home on TV probably see them better.

3. Football involves knocking down a player who is trying to carry the ball down the field. Although players wear a lot of padding and other **protective** gear, injuries are fairly common. **Versions** of the game that involve less physical **contact**—flag football and touch football—are played by teams enjoying the sport just for fun and exercise.

4. As a spectator sport, football is extremely popular, especially among men. Women sometimes call themselves "football **widows**" because, during the football season, their boyfriends or husbands are either at the stadium or **glued** to the TV set. Both college football (played on Saturday afternoons) and professional football (played on Sunday afternoons and Monday nights) attract huge audiences. At the end of the college football season, the best teams **compete** in Bowl games. The day's festivities are colorful and exciting, involving **parades** with floats and marching bands. Bowl games attract huge crowds and big TV audiences. The professional football season ends with the Super Bowls, the game between the country's top two teams. More than 130 million people **worldwide** watch it on TV. It is the most watched TV show in the world. Because of this huge audience, **advertisers** pay about $2 million for a 30-second advertisement!

5. **Note** that the game Americans call football is not what Europeans call football. To Americans, that game is **soccer**. Soccer, the world's most popular sport, the national sport of most European and Latin American countries, has not been a great success in the U.S. as a professional sport. However, it is one of the fastest-growing team sports in U.S. elementary and high schools and is also a popular college sport.

6. While baseball and football are played outdoors (or in huge enclosed stadiums), basketball is the world's most popular indoor sport. **Variations** of the game are also played informally outdoors. Nearly every park in the U.S. has a basketball net and hard-surface playing area, and many American homes have a basketball net outdoors. In NBA, there are 30 professional men's teams. In addition, women's professional basketball has been growing in popularity. Basketball is also played competitively by high school and college students.

7. Professional basketball players make almost impossible **shots** look easy and graceful. Michael Jordan, the former Chicago Bulls player, became famous worldwide because of his achievements on the basketball **court**. Jordan's 13-year career earnings (his salary for playing plus earnings for endorsing products in ads) **exceeded** $300 million! Is it any wonder that almost every tall American boy hopes to grow much taller and eventually play professional basketball?

Other Popular Sports

8. Americans know that **athletics** is good for the body and the mind. Those

who are serious about exercising can find all kinds of activities to do, everything from winter sports to water sports. Some are safe, tame, and not very **strenuous**. Others require speed and great **endurance**. Some even require courage. Many Americans spend a lot of money on equipment and instruction to **participate** in sports they enjoy. Others talk about exercising more but never get around to it.

9. One sport that can be played from about age 10 to 110 is golf. This popular sport is played all year except when the ground is covered with snow. Doctors highly **recommend** it for **mild** exercise, and they often practice what they **preach**. "Don't get sick on a Wednesday," people joke. That's doctors' traditional day off, and supposedly they are all on the golf **course**. The achievements of American golfer Tiger Woods have been an **inspiration** to golfers everywhere. He won the

Masters Tournament in 1997, at the age of 21, and is still **ranked** the world's best golfer. He is also a one-man representative of American multiculturalism. His ethnic background is a **blend** of African-American, Native American, Chinese, European, and Thai!

10. Another sport that is not extremely strenuous and **appeals** to a wide age range is bowling. About 43 million people bowl in the U.S. Many bowling leagues (groups of teams that compete against each other) are formed by coworkers or members of community organizations.

11. Tennis, played by millions throughout the world, is also popular in the U.S. It is played all year, indoors or out, and provides a very **vigorous workout**. When two people are playing against each other, it is called singles; when four play (two teams of two players each), it is called doubles. As with other major sports, top professional tennis players win a lot of money and become famous.

12. Americans also enjoy winter sports on snow or ice. Skiing attracts both individuals and families. In flatter areas of the country, "mountains" are artificially created and covered with **artificial** snow. Skiers also go to **resorts** with real mountains in places such as Aspen, Colorado. Ice-skating, indoors and outdoors, is also popular. Hockey (the national sport of Canada) is a popular team sport for boys in the U.S., too. Girls, however, are more likely to enjoy figure skating.

13. The next category of sports is called **extreme** sports. These are risky activities involving speed, high skill, and danger. They include **daredevil** tricks on snowboards, skateboards, and bicycles; parachute jumps off bridges or cliffs; bungee jumping; barefoot waterskiing; and skydiving. Most Americans consider extreme sports **enthusiasts** extremely foolish. However, others see them as carrying on the traditional pioneering, adventurous spirit that enabled Americans to conquer a wilderness.

After You Read

Knowledge Focus

1. **Consider the following questions.**
    1) What are the three most popular team sports in the U.S.?
    2) What's the difference between Bowl games and the Super Bowl?
    3) What sport may be the doctors' favorite game?
    4) Why are some people crazy about extreme sports?

2. **Match the sports with the associated items.**

   A. baseball   a. extreme sport
   B. football   b. mild exercise
   C. basketball   c. national pastime
   D. golf   d. the Super Bowl
   E. bungee jumping   e. popular indoor sport

Language Focus

1. **Underline the phrase that means the same as the one quoted from the reading.**
    1) "spectator sports and participatory sports"
        a) sports to watch and sports to play
        b) team sports and individual sports
    2) "professional baseball"
        a) played by teams that get paid to play
        b) played for enjoyment
    3) "physical contact"
        a) running a lot
        b) touching each other
    4) "endorsing products"
        a) buying particular products

b) saying in an ad that the particular products are good

5) "Is it any wonder?"

   a) It shouldn't really be surprising.

   b) Do you ever want to know?

2. With a partner, write a correct word to make the meaning of the phrase opposite to the one listed.

   Example:

   a small audience / a ___huge___ audience

   1) the team sports / the _____ sports

   2) an amateur team / a _____ team

   3) real, natural snow / _____ snow

   4) strenuous sports / _____ sports

   5) mental activity / _____ activity

   6) participants in a game / _____ of a game (people watching it)

3. Write the corresponding letter of the correct phrase to complete the sentence.

   1) Baseball is called the national pastime because it _____.

      a) is a very popular sport throughout the U.S.

      b) was very popular in the past

   2) If doctors practice what they preach, they _____.

      a) do what they advise others to do

      b) give a lot of speeches

   3) People who work out a lot _____.

      a) have an outdoor job

      b) exercise often

   4) Many people talk about exercising more but never get around to it, because they _____.

      a) have to deal with some more important matters

      b) dare not to have a try

4. Proofreading and error correction.

   The passage contains FIVE errors. Each indicated line contains a maximum of ONE error. In each case, only ONE word is involved.

In the U.S., basketball remains the team sport most associating with blacks, but white players are at a premium. Teams in certain markets will often endeavor to encourage a white player of limited abilities to come to their team with the hope that the	1) _____ 2) _____

(continued)

largely white crowds will identify with a player. Such players will also generally receive disproportionate large salaries. However, the success of players like Magic Johnson, Julius Erving and, above all, Michael Jordan have diminished this tendency. It remains to be seen whether these players have the same success after the game in coaching and ownership.

(continued)

3) _____

4) _____

5) _____

Comprehensive Work

1. **Share ideas with your team members.**
   How do you prefer to spend your leisure time?
   Read the list of leisure-time activities and decide which you enjoy most. Number them in order of importance, with number 1 as your favorite choice. Share your list with your partner and then with another pair of students.

   _____ Go on a walk or hike   _____ Go swimming
   _____ Work out at a gym   _____ Watch a game
   _____ Read a good book   _____ Listen to music
   _____ Go shopping   _____ Play a sport with friends
   _____ Watch TV   _____ Have a friend visit you

2. **Give an oral presentation on the following topic.**
   Who is your favorite American Sports star?
   Why do you worship him or her?
   What is so special about him or her?

3. **Write an essay on the following topic.**
   Many American children are very impressed by sports stars like Michael Jordan. Do you think sports super stars have a responsibility to be positive role models for young people? Write an essay explaining why or why not, and give examples.

Read More

Text B　　All-American Football

Scanning for details: read the following passage and finish the exercises.

1. In football, the team with the ball tries to get it _____.
    a. in a basket   b. over their goal   c. to the other team's goal

2. Rugby was started in England in _____.
    a. 1839   b. 1874   c. 1905

3. President Roosevelt threatened to stop football because it was getting too _____.
    a. popular   b. dangerous   c. noisy

4. Football originated with _____.
    a. basketball   b. soccer   c. baseball

5. A football game is divided into _____.
    a. two halves   b. three thirds   c. four quarters

Football is not just a game in America. It is an event. A big event. Millions of people attend football games or watch them on television. Thousands of others play football themselves, on professional, school, or neighborhood teams, or just with friends. The games are often only a part of the colorful spectacles that go with them. Parades and marching bands, cheerleaders, and cheering fans with banners and horns are all a part of the festivity surrounding football.

Football has its beginning in soccer and rugby. All have the same objective, which is to get the ball to the opponent's goal and score points. Soccer was played in England in the 11th century. The ball was advanced only by kicking it. In 1839, rugby was born when a frustrated English soccer player picked up the ball and ran down the field with it. Soccer was played by

American college students in the 1800s, but the game was called "football." Then, in 1874, a new form of the football game developed that combined both soccer and rugby. Players not only kicked the ball but advanced it by running with it and passing it to teammates.

American football developed into a rough contact sport. Because protective equipment was not used in those days, it was quite dangerous. In 1905, 18 players were killed and 159 seriously injured. President Roosevelt threatened to ban football if the roughness did not stop. The rules committee began changing the rules and eventually football developed into the game as it is today.

The basic idea of football is very simple. The team that has the ball runs with it or throws or kicks it toward the other team's goal. Each time the team reaches the other's goal, it scores a certain number of points. The other team tries to stop them. They want to get the ball so that they can score. The team that scores the most points wins the game.

The teams play for one hour, divided into four quarters. There is always a halftime break of at least 15 minutes. The teams are allowed timeouts, which are times when the clock is stopped and the team can get together to talk about strategy. The clock is also stopped when players are injured and when there are penalties given out for playing against the rules. Sometimes new players are substituted for those who have already played. There are also breaks for television commercials. With all this going on, the one-hour game can easily take up to two and a half or three hours!

Text C   Air Jordan Walks Away

A 107—87 defeat to 76ers puts an end to superstar's glittering 15-year career.

Michael Jordan finally found the strength to walk off the basketball court, leaving behind the sport he describes as a lover and best friend after playing his final game.

The 40-year-old superstar concluded his fabled 15-year National Basketball Association career in defeat (April 16, 2003) when Philadelphia 76ers beat his Washington Wizards 107—87. But the game was secondary to Jordan's third and final retirement from the game he loved like no player before him, a sport that rewarded his devotion with six NBA titles, two Olympic gold medals and a legendary global legacy.

Jordan led the Chicago Bulls to six NBA titles. He was named the season MVP five times and won the NBA scoring title a record 10 times. Jordan has retired twice before only to return, but at age 40 and no longer be able to dominate games single-handedly, he has said he is "100 percent sure" this was his farewell performance in the game he will forever love. "Love is a very delicate thing," Jordan said. "Once you love it, you  will never lose the love for the game. You never know when you can walk away from it. I tried a couple of times." Jordan's first retirement was in 1993. It ended in 1995 after an ill-fated fling with baseball. After three more titles, he departed again in 1999, only to return a year later as the Wizard's top executive. He was back on the court 18 months later. "Each time I tried to put a time frame on when this love affair was going to be over between basketball and me. And I don't think it ever will. It's just that I got strong enough to say I need to move away from it."

Jordan left no doubt that he will not make yet another comeback. In his final game, Jordan scored 15 points, the last of them on a free throw with 1:45 to play. He was pulled from the game a moment later, taking a seat on the bench while a sell-out crowd of 21,257 gave a three-minute standing ovation.

Jordan scored Washington's first four points in the third quarter but spend most of the fourth quarter on the bench, prompting fans to chant "We Want Mike" as they hungered for one final glance at Jordan on the court. Their persistence was rewarded when Jordan returned to the court with 2:35 remaining to a standing ovation, the crowd ignoring the remainder of the blowout to thrill at his final touches.

Thank Jordan for all the magic moments and memories.

Finish the exercises.

1. Matching

    A. put an end   a. have control of
    B. leave behind   b. most valuable player
    C. single-handedly   c. great applause or cheering
    D. ovation   d. National Basketball Association
    E. dominate   e. end
    F. NBA   f. take leave of
    G. MVP   g. by one person

2. True or False
   a) Jordan concluded his career as a basketball player in a game of victory. _____
   b) Probably Jordan will come back again after retirement for the third time. _____
   c) Jordan was named the season MVP five times and won the NBA scoring title a record 10 times. _____

Notes

Denis Waitley (1933—   ) is one of America's most respected authors, keynote lecturers and productivity consultants on high performance human achievement. With over 10 million audio programs sold in 14 languages, he is one of the most listened-to voices on personal and career success. He is the author of 15 non-fiction books, including several international best sellers, *Seeds of Greatness*, *Being the Best*, *The Winner's Edge*, *The Joy of Working*, and *Empires of the Mind*. His audio album, "The Psychology of Winning," is the all-time best selling program on self-mastery.

For Fun

Book to Read

Michael Mandelbaum: *The Meaning of Sports: Why Americans Watch Baseball, Football, and Basketball and What They See When They Do*

The author, a well respected foreign policy analyst, explores Americans' fascination with team sports and how they satisfy deep human needs.

Movies to See

A League of Their Own

Two sisters join the first female professional baseball league and struggle to help it succeed amidst their own growing competitiveness.

Miracle

The true story of Herb Brooks, the player-turned-coach who led the 1980 U.S. Olympic hockey team to victory over the seemingly unbeatable Soviet Union team.

Songs to Enjoy

R. Kelly: **"I Believe I Can Fly"**

If I can see it, then I can do it, if I just believe it, there is nothing to it...

"Hand in Hand"

Hand in hand we can, start to understand, breaking down the walls that come between us for all time...

Unit 13
The Charm of American Screens

> The remarkable thing about television is that it permits several million people to laugh at the same joke and still feel lonely.
> —T. S. Eliot
>
> Whoever controls the media—the images—controls the culture.
> —Allen Ginsberg

Unit Goals

- To take a general look at American entertainment media
- To get acquainted with some types of American TV programs
- To recognize the role of entertainment media in Americans' life
- To develop critical thinking and intercultural communication skills
- To learn useful words and expressions on American entertainment media and improve English language skills

Before You Read

1. **Brainstorm**: Discuss and share ideas with your partner.
   1) List four reasons why you like American movies:
      _____, _____,
      _____, _____.
   2) List four reasons why you dislike American movies:
      _____, _____,
      _____, _____.

2. Can you tell what movies the lines are from?
   1) Mama always said life was like a box of chocolates, you never know what you're gonna get. _____
   2) I'm going to make him an offer he can't refuse. _____
   3) After all, tomorrow is another day! _____
   4) I have to remind myself that some birds aren't meant to be caged. Their feathers are just too bright. _____
   5) Look, Simba. Everything the light touches is our kingdom. _____
   6) You're gonna go on and you're gonna make lots of babies, and you're gonna die an old, old lady warm in her bed. _____

Start to Read

Text A Entertainment Media in the U. S.

1. By far, the most popular leisure-time activity is watching television in America. There is at least one TV set in 98% of American **households**, and many have two or three. About 82% of American homes have a videocassette recorder (VCR), which is capable of recording and playing back TV shows or movies.

2. What's on TV? Afternoon programming **consists** mostly of game shows, talk shows, and never-ending dramas commonly called **soap operas**. For children, daytime TV offers clever programs that educate while entertaining. There are also a lot of **cartoons**. At dinner time, news is **broadcast**. Evening entertainment consists mostly of situation comedies (sitcoms) which **portray** some aspects of life (families, singles, seniors, and so on) in a **humorous** way. There are also  movies, adventure shows, dramas, and various weekly shows with the same cast of characters and general theme but a different story each week.

3. For those who want more TV than the free stations provide, cable TV is **available** in most parts of the country. To receive cable TV, one must pay a monthly **subscription** fee. Wires are **attached** to the TV set to enable the

subscriber to receive the cable broadcasts. Cable channels tend to **specialize** in one type of program. There are stations for news, sports, movies, music videos, business, health, history, and arts.

4. TV, at its best, is entertaining and educational. However, there are two problems. Most viewers watch too much, and the quality (especially on the free stations) is often poor. How much is too much? Studies **indicate** that the average American watches TV about 28 hours a week. (Children watch about 20 hours; older women are up to 42 hours.) According to one study in 1950, American 14-year-olds had a vocabulary of 25,000 words, but today's children at the same age know only 10,000 words. The reason for the **decrease** may be that TV takes up a lot of leisure time kids once spent reading. Besides, the other effect of watching so much TV also seems to be shortening children's **attention span**. Since the **advent** of the **remote control** device and the **proliferation** of channels, many watchers like to "**graze**" from one program to the next, or "**channel surf**"—constantly clicking the remote control to change from channel to channel, stopping for only a few seconds to see if something catches their attention.

5. Some people spend much of their free time lying on the couch watching TV and eating **junk food**. They are called "**couch potatoes**," because they are

nothing but "eyes." (The small marks on potatoes are called eyes.) Couch potatoes would rather watch a baseball game on TV than go to play softball in the park with friends, or even go to a movie. Cable and satellite TV bring hundreds of stations into American homes, and there is an almost limitless choice of programs. Technology will continue to offer **consumers** bigger

TV screens and clearer pictures at **affordable** prices. Moreover, TV of the future will be more **interactive**. Better technical quality may encourage viewers to watch even more—and, some say, become even less physically fit and more **overweight**.

6. And what about quality? On the **commercial** networks especially, many shows are silly, **trite**, in poor taste, or extremely violent. By the age of 18, the typical American has seen 40,000 killings on TV and in movies **combined**. Does all this **fake bloodshed** cause some teens to commit real violent crimes?

Some people think there is a connection. American TV has **earned** the insulting **nickname** "**idiot box**." But for those who want to avoid either too much TV or bad TV, the solution is simple: Click the "off" button.

7. Movies are another common source of entertainment, viewed in theaters or at home. TV stations show movies, and there is a store that rents videotapes or DVDs in just about every neighborhood. Americans **consume** movies in great quantities, and movie stars become public **idols**. Once a year, the movie industry gives out a whole series of honors to movie-makers. Nearly a billion people worldwide watch this televised awards **presentation**—the Academy Awards.

8. Other popular sources of entertainment are recordings and radio. Sales of recordings in all forms **exceed** $12 billion annually, with **compact discs** by far the most popular **medium**. Radio, too, has its place in the American entertainment scene. It is a great companion in the car, on the treadmill, or on the jogging trail.

After You Read

Knowledge Focus

1. Discuss with your partner on the following questions.
   1) What are some of the popular programs on American TV screen?
   2) What are the two problems about TV watching in America?
   3) What effects has TV brought to children in America?
   4) What is a "couch potato"? Please give further description in your own words.

2. Find the details from the passage to fill in the blanks.
   1) There is at least one TV set in _____ of American households, and many have two or three.
   2) Afternoon programming consists mostly of game shows, talk shows, and never-ending dramas commonly called _____.
   3) For those who want more TV than the free stations provide, _____ TV is available in most parts of the country.
   4) Since the advent of the _____ device and the proliferation of channels, many watchers like to "graze" from one program to the next, or "channel surf."
   5) Nearly a billion people worldwide watch this televised awards presentation—the _____.
   6) Sales of recordings in all forms exceed $12 billion annually, with _____ by far

the most popular medium.

Language Focus

1. Underline the phrase that means the same as the one quoted from the reading.

    1) Afternoon programming *consists* mostly *of* game shows, talk shows, and never-ending dramas commonly called soap operas.

       a) is composed of

       b) makes up of

    2) The reason for the decrease may be that TV *takes up* a lot of leisure time kids once spent reading.

       a) begins or starts to do

       b) occupies, uses

    3) Some people spend much of their free time lying on the couch watching TV and eating *junk food*.

       a) food that is thought to be good for losing weight

       b) food that is thought to be bad for health

    4) *Couch potatoes* would rather watch a baseball game on TV than go play softball in the park with friends.

       a) people addicted to TV

       b) people glued to the comfort of sofa

    5) Many TV watchers like to "graze" from one program to the next, or "*channel surf*."

       a) watch several programs at once

       b) change from one channel to another quickly

2. Complete the following sentences with the proper words and expressions listed below.

portray	consumer	annually	earn
combine	exceed	affordable	proliferation
advent	subscribe	attach	indicate

    1) At least 200,000 people graduate from universities and colleges and secondary vocational schools _____.

    2) I _____ to a number of journals concerned with my subject.

    3) Most actors _____ Hamlet as an unhappy man, lacking in the power of decision.

    4) People are much better informed since the _____ of television.

    5) Health-conscious _____ want more information about the food they buy.

    6) Our generosity shall never _____ our means.

    7) Measures should be taken to prevent the _____ of weapons of mass destruction.

    8) She stopped at nothing to _____ money.

    9) A red sky at night often _____ fine weather the next day.

    10) They will _____ their two companies against their competitors.

11) With lower prices, flats have become more _____ to genuine home buyers.

12) We should _____ primary importance to the development of economy.

3. **Fill in each blank with a suitable preposition or adverb.**

   1) About 82% of American homes have a videocassette recorder, which is capable _____ recording and playing back TV shows or movies.

   2) What's _____ TV? Afternoon programming consists mostly _____ game shows, talk shows, and never-ending dramas.

   3) Wires are attached _____ the TV set to enable the subscriber to receive the cable broadcasts.

   4) The reason for the decrease may be that TV takes _____ a lot of leisure time kids once spent reading.

   5) Technology will continue to offer consumers bigger TV screens and clearer pictures _____ affordable prices.

   6) Americans consume movies _____ great quantities, and movie stars become public idols.

   7) Once a year, the movie industry gives _____ a whole series of honors to movie-makers.

4. **Proofreading and error correction.**

   The passage contains FIVE errors. Each indicated line contains a maximum of ONE error. In each case, only ONE word is involved.

The talk show as a broad generic category is one of the oldest and most durable electronic media forms, with roots dated back to the early days of radio in the U.S. Quite simply, talk shows are performative conversations featuring host and some combination of experts, celebrities or "average citizens." They cover wide array of subjects including news, politics, current events, sports, religion, hobbies, the arts, gossip, tips for home-makers, self-help therapy, and as well as advice. As Rose notes, although it appears to be the loosest and most casual of genres, the talk show is carefully and purposefully crafted, based on the concept of "controlled spontaneity" and adhered to a predictable progression of situations and segments.	1) _____ 2) _____ 3) _____ 4) _____ 5) _____

Comprehensive Work

1. Act It Out with Your Partner!

From the movie *Roman Holiday*—A bored and sheltered princess escapes her guardians and falls in love with an American newsman in Rome...

Joe: (*Cheerfully*) Good morning.
Ann: (*She starts; in a low, worried tone*) Where's Doctor Bonnachoven?
Joe: (*Unbothered*) Er, I'm afraid I don't know anybody by that name.
Ann: (*Puzzled*) Wasn't I talking to him just now?
Joe: 'Fraid not.
Ann: (*Suddenly frightened; feeling herself beneath the sheets*) Have—have I had an accident?
Joe: No.
Ann: (*Reassured*) Quite safe for me to sit up, huh?
Joe: Yeah, (*bending down to her*) perfect. (*He lifts her pillow back and helps her sit up, leaning against it. She looks at him all the while, not fully trusting of him. Joe leans against the cupboard at the foot of the bed.*)
Ann: Thank you. (*He smiles back. She looks down at her pajamas, then to Joe.*) Are these yours? (*He nods. Ann, suddenly panicked, feels under the sheets for her pajamas bottoms.*)
Joe: Er, did—did you lose something?
Ann: (*Smiling, relieved*) No. No. (*Politely, suppressing her anxiety*) W—would you be so kind as to tell me w—where I am?
Joe: Well, this is what is laughingly known as my apartment.
Ann: (*Concerned; rising suddenly*) Did you bring me here by force?
Joe: No, no, no... (*Smiling*) quite the contrary.
Ann: Have I been here all night... alone?
Joe: (*Smiling*) If you don't count me, yes.
Ann: (*Seriously*) So I've spent the night here—with you.
Joe: (*Hurrying to reassure her*) Oh, well, now, I—I don't know if I'd use those words exactly, but er, from a certain angle, yes.
(*Ann looks down, thinking. After a moment, reassured that everything is alright after all, laughs.*)
Ann: (*Presenting her hand*) How do you do?
Joe: (*Shaking her hand*) How do you do?
Ann: And you are?
Joe: Bradley, Joe Bradley.
Ann: Delighted.

Joe: You don't know how delighted I am to meet you.

Ann: (*Gesturing to the chair to her left.*) You may sit down.

Joe: Well, thank you very much. (*He sits down on the bed instead; she pulls back her legs, looking back at him like a frightened gazelle.*) What's your name?

Ann: (*She pauses, stalling*) Er...you may call me Anya.

Joe: Thank you, Anya. (*Cheerfully; rising to go to the table*) Would you like a cup of coffee?

Ann: What time is it?

Joe: Oh, about one thirty.

Ann: (*Panicked*) One thirty! (*Jumping out of bed towards the door*) I must get dressed and go! (*Remembering, she grabs the blankets to cover herself.*)

Joe: (*Casually; continuing to prepare the coffee*) Why? What's your hurry? There's lots of time.

Ann: Oh no, there isn't and I've—I've been quite enough trouble to you as it is.

Joe: Trouble? (*Smiling*) You're not what I'd call trouble.

Ann: (*Pleased*) I'm not?

Joe: (*Going to the bathroom door*) I'll run a bath for you.

2. Give an oral presentation on the following topic.

Tell your classmates something about your favorite films or movie stars. What are so special about them? What have you learned from them?

3. Essay Writing.

What changes has TV brought to people's life? Are you happy with the changes?

Read More

Text B **Hollywood: How the American Movie Industry Was Born**

Scanning for details: read the following passage and finish the exercises.

1. Hollywood is located in the city of _____.

   a. New York   b. Washington D.C.   c. Los Angeles

2. The very first movie to be filmed in Hollywood was _____.

   a. Gone with the Wind   b. In Old California   c. Cleopatra

As a district in Los Angeles in the western United States, Hollywood pretty much encompasses what the American film and television industry is all about. Probably all functions that are required to make a film product can be found in this one location. This includes filming in studios, film editing, post-production and even casting of actors.

Hollywood is every actor's dream. It has given fame and fortune to many  names and faces for almost a century. The place has produced hundreds of hit movies, making it the movie capital of the world. This is one of the reasons why many aspiring actors across America try their luck out in Hollywood. They gain quite a decent living out of acting for films and various TV shows that are produced there.

The name Hollywood was already existent long before it became synonymous with being a movie powerhouse. In fact, Hollywood would not be what it is if it was not for a small troop of actors that ventured into it in 1910. The place was a small village just north of Los Angeles. The very first movie to be filmed there was *In Old California*. After rumors spread out that California was such a great place to shoot movies, directors from all over America began to bring their projects out west into Hollywood. This is how the American Movie Industry was born.

Today, most motion picture productions still happen in and about Hollywood. But major picture houses have had to build their properties in other places surrounding Hollywood because of the lack of real estate. At present, the only studio left within the limits of Hollywood is Paramount Studios. Other landmarks that can be found are the Kodak Theater and the Hollywood Hotel, which is now home to the famous Oscars. The famous Hollywood Walk of Fame can also be found there. Honorees receive a star based on their lifetime as actors and that star is placed into the ground on the walkway. It forever immortalizes them as key contributors to the success of the film industry.

Aside from being the film industry's powerhouse in movie making and television programming, Hollywood is also home to many venues and theaters that host award shows like the Academy Awards. It is popular among tourists and is known to have one of the best nightlife recreation facilities in the world.

For the tourists, they also make their way around the area hoping just to catch a glimpse of their favorite stars that are more than likely to appear on the streets. Music studios have also set up their businesses in Hollywood. One of the most famous companies is Capitol Records on Vine Street. So aside from the growing number of actors and actresses, there is also room for musicians to make their mark in entertainment. And entertainment is what Hollywood is all about.

Text C American Soap Operas

A **soap opera** is an ongoing, episodic work of fiction, usually broadcast on television or radio. Programs described as soap operas have existed as an entertainment long enough for audiences to recognize them simply by the term **soap**. The name *soap opera* stems from the original dramatic serials broadcast on radio that had soap manufacturers such as Procter and Gamble, Colgate-Palmolive, and Lever Brothers as the show's sponsors. These early radio serials were broadcast in weekday daytime slots when mostly housewives would be available to listen; thus the shows were aimed at and consumed by a predominantly female audience.

The term "soap opera" has at times been generally applied to any romantic serial, but is also used to describe the more naturalistic, unglamorous evening, prime-time drama serials of the UK such as *Coronation Street*. What differentiates a soap from other television drama programs is the open-ended nature of the narrative, with stories spanning several episodes. The defining feature that makes a program a soap opera is that it, according to Albert Moran, is "that form of television that works with a continuous open narrative. Each episode ends with a promise that the storyline is to be continued in another episode." Soap opera stories run concurrently, intersect, and lead into further developments. An individual episode of a soap opera will generally switch between several different concurrent story threads that may at times interconnect and affect one another, or may run entirely independent of each other. Each episode may feature some of the show's current storylines but

not always all of them. There is some rotation of both storylines and actors so any given storyline or actor will appear in some but usually not all of a week's worth of episodes. Soap operas generally avoid bringing all the current storylines to a conclusion at the same time. When one storyline ends, there are always several other story threads at differing stages of development. Soap opera episodes typically end on some sort of cliffhanger.

Evening soap operas sometimes differ from this general format and are more likely to feature the entire cast in each episode, and to represent all current storylines in each episode. Additionally, evening soap operas and other serials that run for only part of the year tend to bring things to a dramatic end of season cliffhanger.

In the U.S., the phrase "soap opera" has also entered the language as a metaphor that can be applied to any narrative, either real or imagined, that appears to be excessively laced with emotion, and contains what appear to be unlikely dramatic twists: "Her life is one big soap opera."

Answer the questions.
1. Have you seen any American soap operas? How do they impress you?
2. Can you list some of the major characteristics of American soap operas? What are they?

Text D Oprah Winfrey

On January 29, 1954 Oprah Gail Winfrey was born to unwed, teenage parents in Kosciusko, Mississippi. Oprah had a mountain of obstacles already in front of her as a newborn baby: She was born to unwed teenage parents, she was female, she was black, and she was poor. Oprah's mother was an eighteen-year-old housemaid named Vernita Lee. Her father was a twenty-year-old doing duty in the armed forces; his name was Vernon Winfrey.

For the first six years of her life, the young Winfrey was raised on a Mississippi farm by her grandmother and that is perhaps the first stroke of good luck for the young child. Oprah has stated that living with her grandmother probably saved her life. While in her grandmother's care, she was taught to read at a very early age, instilling a love of reading in her that she retains today. She began her public speaking career at the tender age of three when she began reading aloud and reciting sermons to the congregation of her church.

Oprah has said that she heard her grandmother state on several occasions that Oprah was "gifted." While the young child did not know exactly what being "gifted" meant, she thought that it meant that she was special. And that was enough to keep her going. That bit of praise, the thought that she was "gifted" and "special" may have been what got her through the hard years that she was to spend with her mother.

At the age of six, her mother, Vernita Lee, decided that she could care for her young daughter and Oprah was sent to live with her mother in Milwaukee. From ages six to thirteen, Oprah stayed with her mother. She was raped by a cousin when she was nine years old and later molested by a male friend of her mother's and by an uncle. The young girl never told anyone about the abuse that she was suffering. Instead, she held her anger and pain inside and she rebelled. She repeatedly ran away and got into trouble.

Her mother decided to put her into a detention home. Fortunately for Oprah, she was denied admission to the home because there were no openings. So, in what may have been her second major stroke of good luck, she was sent to live with her father Vernon Winfrey in Nashville. Before she ceased her promiscuous and wild behavior, she became pregnant and gave birth to a stillborn baby boy when she was fourteen. The death of her baby devastated her and she vowed to turn her life around.

Her father helped her with her mission by strapping her with his strict rules and discipline. Vernon made sure that his daughter stuck to her curfew, maintained high grades in school and encouraged Oprah to be her best. Oprah's father helped her turn her life around. Oprah has spoke of his requirement that she read a book each week and complete a book report on the book.

At the age of nineteen, Oprah landed her first job as a reporter for a radio station in Nashville. Shortly afterwards, she entered Tennessee State University to pursue a career in radio and television broadcasting. During her freshman year at TSU, Oprah won several pageants, including "Miss Black Nashville" and "Miss Tennessee."

In 1976, Oprah Winfrey moved to Baltimore, where she hosted a TV

show called *People Are Talking*. The show was a hit and Winfrey stayed for eight years. She was then recruited by a TV station in Chicago to host her own morning show, *A. M. Chicago*. The show was competing against the immensely popular *Phil Donahue Show*. After several months, Oprah's warm-hearted style had taken her to the first place in the ratings. Her success led to a role in Steven Spielberg's film, *The Color Purple* in 1985, for which she was nominated for an Academy Award.

In 1986, Oprah started the *Oprah Winfrey Show*. The rest is, as they say, history. Oprah has come from being a poor, black, farm girl from Mississippi to a national celebrity. To her resume she can add reporter, actress, writer, producer, activist and TV talk show host... but it does not stop there. Oprah, it seems, is unstoppable.

Finish the exercises.

1. Matching

   A. unwed   a. locking-up
   B. congregation   b. loose, immoral
   C. molest   c. worshippers
   D. detention   d. extremely upset
   E. promiscuous   e. not married
   F. devastated   f. famous person
   G. celebrity   g. physically abused

2. Arrange the following events in chronological order and mark the events with numbers.

   ___ Oprah's mother decided that she could care for her young daughter and Oprah was sent to live with her mother in Milwaukee.

   ___ Oprah won several pageants, including "Miss Black Nashville" and "Miss Tennessee."

   ___ Oprah was sent to live with her father Vernon Winfrey in Nashville.

   ___ Oprah started the *Oprah Winfrey Show*.

   ___ Oprah played a role in Steven Spielberg's film, *The Color Purple*.

   ___ The young Winfrey lived together with her grandmother on a Mississippi farm.

   ___ Oprah Winfrey moved to Baltimore, where she hosted a TV show called *People Are Talking*.

Proper Names

Mississippi	n.	密西西比(美国州名)
Nashville	n.	纳什维尔(美国田纳西州首府)
Tennessee	n.	田纳西(美国州名)
Baltimore	n.	巴尔的摩(美国马里兰州一港口城市)

Know More

Some Major U.S. News & Cable Networks

ABC—American Broadcasting Company
CBS—Columbia Broadcasting System
NBC—National Broadcasting Company
PBS—Public Broadcasting Service
CNN—Cable News Network
MTV—Music Television
SC—Sports Channel
TDC—The Discovery Channel
USA—USA Network
DIS—The Disney Channel
CNBC—Consumer News and Business Channel

Notes

1. **T. S. Eliot** (1888—1965) with full name as Thomas Stearns Eliot, was a poet, dramatist, and literary critic. He received the Nobel Prize in Literature in 1948. He wrote the poems *The Love Song of J. Alfred Prufrock*, *The Waste Land*, *The Hollow Men*, *Ash Wednesday* and *Four Quartets*; the plays *Murder in the Cathedral* and *The Cocktail Party*; and the essay "Tradition and the Individual Talent."
2. **Allen Ginsberg** (1926—1997) was an American poet. Ginsberg is best known for the poem *Howl* (1956), celebrating his friends of the Beat Generation and attacking what he saw as the destructive forces of materialism and conformity in the United States at the time.

Movies and TV Series to Watch

The Truman Show
An insurance adjuster discovers his entire life is actually a TV show...

Friends
The lives, loves, and laughs of six young friends living in Manhattan.

Grey's Anatomy
A drama centered on the personal and professional lives of five surgical interns and their supervisors.

Everybody Loves Raymond
It never stops for successful sports writer Ray Barone, whose oddball family life consists of a fed-up wife, overbearing parents, and an older brother with lifelong jealousy.

Unit 14

The Music of America

> If I were not a physicist, I would probably be a musician. I often think in music. I live my daydreams in music. I see my life in terms of music.
>
> —Albert Einstein

Unit Goals

- To recognize different types of music in America
- To learn to appreciate the typical American music
- To get acquainted with some great figures in the history of American music
- To develop critical thinking and intercultural communication skills
- To learn useful words and expressions concerning American music and improve English language skills

Before You Read

1. Consider the following questions.
   1) Does music mean a lot to you? If so, what do you benefit from music?
   2) What kind of music do you like the best? Why?
   3) How much do you know about American music? Talk about it with your partner.

2. Match the following songs with the singers.
   1) "Heal the World"   a. Madonna
   2) "What a Wonderful World"   b. Elvis Presley
   3) "Take Me Home Country Road"   c. Bob Dylan
   4) "Can't Help Falling in Love" d. Michael Jackson
   5) "Girl from the North Country" e. Louis Armstrong
   6) "Don't Cry for Me, Argentina" f. John Denver

Text A The Music of America

The Sound of Country Music

1. Put together a guitar, singer, simple music, and **sentimental** words, and you have got country music. The sound is uniquely American. But like so much in this land of immigrants, it is a **combination** of the past and the present, the borrowed and invented. Its deepest roots are in faraway places, in the music brought here by people seeking a new life. The people changed over time and so did country music. But it has never lost its special sound like jazz and early rock and roll. Country music is the music of America. It **reflects** the hearts and minds and soul of its people.

2. The history of country music is hundreds of years old. It is older than America itself. It begins with the immigrants from Scotland and Ireland who brought their traditional songs and **instruments** to the New World. Many went to a southeastern mountain area called Appalachia. These settlers played their bagpipes (a wind instrument) and lutes (pear-shaped stringed instruments). They sang the songs and **ballads** of their homelands. Eventually, however, the **lyrics** changed. There were new stories to tell, new troubles and heartaches to mourn. There were also new loves to sing about. New instruments started to be used too. They were **stringed instruments** such as zithers, fiddles, guitars, and banjos.

3. As the settlers spread to the South and West, the music of Appalachia went with them. It changed form **slightly** with the new environments and new influences. It gave birth to what became known as country music. This was the real folk music of **rural** America. It was a basic, simple music with songs about love and grief, heartache and death. It was sung at family **gatherings** and on back porches. But **eventually** it was recorded and heard on radios in the South.

4. People continued to **migrate** west to California from Oklahoma and Texas. They also went north to cities like Detroit, Chicago, Cleveland, and Baltimore. Again, they took their music with them. Then there were new songs about life in the city and about the railroads that brought them there and connected them with their lives "back home." These songs had titles like

"Dallas," "Streets of Baltimore," "Saginaw, Michigan," and "New York City Blues." Time went by and cities and towns spread out across America. New influences continued to change country music. It was recorded, performed, and heard in more and more places.

5. Today, the sound of country music can be heard throughout the land. It has **incorporated** many styles of music like jazz, rock and roll, even Mexican and Hawaiian music. Songs have a much broader range of subjects. However, love and heartache, as in most popular music, are sung about the most. Some people do not like these changes. They think country music is not "pure" any more, that it has gone too far from its **original** sound. But music of all kinds has always been a reflection of society. Since its mountain beginnings, country music has shown the changing face of America, the **transitions** from one generation to another. Times have changed and so has country music. If anything, it is more popular than ever, yet it remains a truly American sound.

Rock and Roll

6. In 1955, rock and roll was born in America. That year, Bill Haley and His Comets performed "Rock Around the Clock," the first big hit of this new style of music. It was first known as "rock and roll" and then simply as "rock." It would become the most popular type of American music from that point on. And it would always appeal to young people as an expression of their search for **identity** and independence.

7. Rock and roll of the mid-1950s grew mainly out of **rhythm** and blues. It was a dance music of African-Americans that combined blues, jazz and **gospel** styles. Rock was also influenced by country and western music. The most successful early rock and roll performer was Elvis Presley. He **reigned** as the "king" of rock and roll for a decade.

8. Just as rock and roll **originated** from a combination of music styles, it developed into many different forms. During the 1960s, rock music was made up of a number of different styles. It ranged from the surf music of the Beach Boys to the hard rock of the Rolling Stones. One of the big differences between the 1960s rock and earlier rock and roll was the use of **electronic instruments** and sound equipment. It was also freer and more **experimental**.

9. British groups played an important part in the development of rock music in the 1960s. The Beatles were the first British group to achieve success in the U.S. Their first hit recordings were "I Want to Hold Your Hand," "Can't

Buy Me Love," and "Love Me Do." Other successful British groups were the Rolling Stones, The Who, and the Animals. Meanwhile in America, San Francisco was becoming the leading center of rock with such groups as Jefferson Airplane and the Grateful Dead.

10. In the 1970s, rock was as popular as ever. Many of the rock groups of the 1960s broke up. Others like the Rolling Stones and Grateful Dead continued to perform and record. The 1970s and early 1980s were years of great technological progress in the production of rock music. **Sophisticated** instruments and recording equipments were used, including tape recorders with several tracks, and synthesizers. Like the 1960s, the 1970s also saw the development of different styles. Heavy metal used extreme **amplification** and long electric guitar **solos**. Some of the best-known heavy-metal rock performers included Alice Cooper, Grand Funk Railroad, and Aerosmith.

11. The rock music of the late 1970s once again **emphasized** the rhythm and energy of early rock and roll. It also helped produce the styles of the 1980s and 1990s. Today rock is still wide open to **diversity**, experimentation, and invention. It is still the music of young people. But today older people who listened to rock when they were young continue to enjoy it. In many ways, rock is a mirror of American culture. It is energetic and **unpredictable**. It is a mixture of styles that work together, and it offers something to people of all ages. It seems Americans will always be rocking round the clock.

After You Read

Knowledge Focus

1. Consider the following questions.

   1) What are the major characteristics of American country music?

   2) Why do some people think country music isn't "pure" any more?

   3) Why does rock and roll appeal to young people so much?

   4) Why do some people say rock and roll is a mirror of American culture?

2. What can you relate to?

   For example: When people mention jazz, I can think of...

cornet, African-American, Louis Armstrong...

1) When people mention American country music, I can think of...
   _____

2) When people mention rock and roll, I can think of...
   _____

3. **Find the details from the passage to fill in the blanks.**
   1) The history of country music begins with the immigrants from _____ and _____ who brought their traditional songs and instruments to the New World.
   2) Songs of country music have a much broader range of subjects nowadays. However, _____ and _____, as in most popular music, are sung about the most.
   3) In _____, rock and roll was born in America. That year Bill Haley and His Comets performed "_____," the first big hit of this new style of music.
   4) The most successful early rock and roll performer was _____. He reigned as the "king" of rock and roll for a decade.
   5) British groups played an important part in the development of rock music in the 1960s. _____ were the first British group to achieve success in the U.S.
   6) Today rock is still wide open to _____, experimentation, and invention. It is still the music of young people as an expression of their search for _____ and _____.

Language Focus
1. **Complete the following sentences with the proper words listed below.**

sentimental	diversity	unpredictable	originate
reign	identity	eventually	incorporate
transition	migrate		

   1) All theories _____ from practice and in turn serve practice.
   2) It's easy to create a phony _____ in cyberspace.
   3) We keep the old clock for _____ reasons; it was a present from my father.
   4) The new car design _____ all the latest safety features.
   5) Mary has a great _____ of interests; she likes sports, travel, photography, and gardening.
   6) She hoped that the problem would _____ pass away.
   7) Some birds _____ to warmer countries in winter.
   8) I find it difficult to rub along with Paul, he's so _____.
   9) Once he is crowned, the king will _____ until he dies.
   10) We need to ensure a smooth _____ between the old system and the new one.

2. **Fill in each blank with a suitable preposition or adverb.**

   1) The music of Appalachia changed form slightly _____ the new environments and new influences. It gave birth _____ what became known as country music.

   2) It was sung _____ family gatherings and on back porches. But eventually it was recorded and heard _____ radios in the South.

   3) Time went _____ and cities and towns spread _____ across America.

   4) "Rock" would become the most popular type of American music and it would always appeal _____ young people.

   5) Rock and roll of the mid-1950s grew mainly _____ _____ rhythm and blues.

   6) Many of the rock groups of the 1960s broke _____. Others like the Rolling Stones and Grateful Dead continued to perform and record.

3. **Proofreading and error correction.**

   The passage contains FIVE errors. Each indicated line contains a maximum of ONE error. In each case, only ONE word is involved.

Perhaps the most lasting effect of post-1960s disillusionment on popular music was a ever-growing strain of irony. Sometimes paralyzing, sometimes revelatory, the irony-suffusing pop exemplified an era is lacking a sense of revolutionary possibility. In much of the popular music of the post-1960s era, irony is a fundamental component, evident in the work of David Bowie, Madonna, David Byrne, Beck, and late even U2. Certainly some massively popular artists have mostly steered clear it. Also, ingenuous pop still has a large audience, as evidenced in the music of Michael Jackson, Debbie Gibson and Whitney Houston. Still, the fact that ironic self-consciousness is one of the key features of pop music is remarkable, given that the category once consisted primarily earnest odes to love and heartbreak.	1) _____ 2) _____ 3) _____ 4) _____ 5) _____

Comprehensive Work

1. **Enjoy a Song.**

   Listen to the song "Love Me Tender" by Elvis Presley. Fill in the lyric blanks first, and try to sing along.

Love Me Tender

Love me tender, love me _____,
Never let me go.
You have made my life _____,
And I love you so.

Love me tender, love me true,
All my dreams _____.
For my darling, I love you,
And I always will.

Love me tender, love me _____,
Take me to your _____.
For it's there that I _____,
And we'll never _____.

Love me tender, love me true,
All my dreams fulfilled.
For my darling, I love you,
And I always will.

Love me tender, love me _____,
Tell me you are mine.
I'll be yours _____ all the years,
Till the end of _____.

Love me tender, love me true,
All my dreams fulfilled.
For my darling, I love you,
And I always will.

2. **Essay Writing.**
   Make full use of your imagination, and describe an ideal world of music.

Read More

Text B The King of Rock 'n' Roll

When Elvis Presley died on August the 16th, 1977, radio and television programs all over the world were interrupted to give the news of his death. President Carter was asked to declare a day of national mourning. Carter said, "Elvis Presley changed the face of American popular culture... He was unique and irreplaceable." Eighty thousand people attended his funeral. The streets were jammed with cars, and Elvis Presley films were shown on television, and his records were played on the radio all day. In the year after his death, one hundred million Presley LPs were sold.

Elvis Presley was born on January the 8th, 1935, in Tupelo, Mississippi. His twin brother, Jesse Garon, died at birth. His parents were very poor and Elvis never had music lessons, but he was surrounded by music from an early age. His parents were very religious, and Elvis regularly sang at church services. In 1948, when he was thirteen, his family moved to Memphis, Tennessee. He left school in 1953 and got a job as a truck driver.

In the summer of 1953, Elvis paid four dollars and recorded two songs for his mother's birthday at Sam Phillips' Sun Records studio. Sam Phillips heard Elvis and asked him to record "That's All Right" in July 1954. Twenty thousand copies were sold, mainly in and around Memphis. He made five more records for Sun, and in July 1955 he met Colonel Tom Parker, who became his manager in November. Parker sold Elvis's contract to RCA

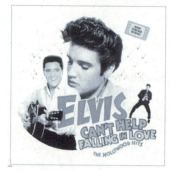

Records. Sun Records got thirty-five thousand dollars and Elvis got five thousand dollars. With the money he bought a pink Cadillac for his mother. On January the 10th, 1956, Elvis recorded "Heartbreak Hotel" and a million copies were sold. In the next fourteen months he made another fourteen records, and they were all big hits. In 1956 he also made his first film in Hollywood.

In March, 1958, Elvis had to join the army. He wanted to be an ordinary soldier. When his hair was cut, thousands of women cried. He spent the next two years in Germany, where he met Priscilla Beaulieu, who became his wife eight years later on May the 1st, 1967. In 1960 he left the army and went to Hollywood where he made several films during the next few years.  By 1968, many people had become tired of Elvis. He had not performed live since 1960. But he recorded a new LP "From Elvis in Memphis" and appeared in a special television program. He became popular again, and went to Las Vegas, where he was paid seven hundred fifty thousand dollars for four weeks. In 1972, his wife left him, and they were divorced in October, 1973. He died from a heart attack. He had been working too hard, and eating and drinking too much for several years. He left all his money to his only daughter, Lisa Marie Presley. She became one of the richest people in the world when she was only nine years old.

So why, after all these years, is the world stuck on Elvis? The answer lies in culture: Elvis Presley is American myth personified. He is greater than the sum of his songs and movies; he symbolizes the American Dream. Born in poverty, Elvis used his innate talent to rise above his condition and achieve his dream, without coming from a socially connected, politically powerful, or wealthy family. He propelled himself from an unknown hillbilly singer to international super-stardom as a rock 'n' roll performer, only to die young and leave behind a growing legion of fans.

Those fans choose to overlook Elvis' drug dependency and other excessive behavior, preferring instead to recall what they see as his better nature. During his lifetime, Elvis donated money to charities and brought gifts for the poor and his family and friends. Furthermore, the hometown boy who made good never left the comfort of Memphis, always keeping close to his roots, remembering the people and places from which he came.

For some, the reasons behind the continued celebration of Elvis's life are not so mythical. So many talents today are one-hit wonders, unable to lay claim as the world's greatest entertainer. Elvis had talent, strength, and charisma. He changed a generation. Sam Phillips, who first recorded Elvis on Sun Records, gives a simple response when asked about Elvis's undying popularity, "Elvis has lasted because he was one of us."

Finish the following exercises.

1. Arrange the following events in chronological order and mark the events with numbers.

    _____ Elvis paid four dollars and recorded two songs for his mother's birthday at Sam Phillips' Sun Records studio.

    _____ Elvis had his hair cut and joined the army.

    _____ Elvis's family moved to Memphis, Tennessee.

    _____ Elvis made his first film in Hollywood.

    _____ Elvis became popular again, and went to Las Vegas, where he was paid seven hundred fifty thousand dollars for four weeks.

    _____ Elvis met Colonel Tom Parker, who became his manager.

2. Why, after all these years, is the world stuck on Elvis?

    Base your understanding on the passage and give an explanation in your own words. And share your understanding with your partner.

Text C Jazz

Scanning for details: read the following passage and finish the following exercises.

1. The music that we call Jazz was born around the year 1895 in _____.

    a. New Jersey　　　b. Louisiana　　　c. New Orleans

2. What made Jazz different from the other earlier forms of music was the use of _____.

    a. rhythm　　　b. improvisation　　　c. instruments

3. Jazz is the cultural "mixed race" offspring of _____ and _____ cultures.

    a. African　　　b. European　　　c. Latin-American

4. _____, a cornet player, is generally considered to be the first real Jazz musician.

    a. Buddy Bolden　　　b. Joe Oliver　　　c. Bunk Johnson

5. _____ soon grew to become one of the greatest and most successful musicians of all time, and later one of the biggest stars in the world.

    a. Kid Ory　　　b. Louis Armstrong　　　c. Charlie Parker

Unit 14　The Music of America

　　The music that we call Jazz was born around the year 1895 in New Orleans. It brought together the elements of ragtime, marching band music, and the blues.

　　What made Jazz different from the other earlier forms of music was the use of improvisation. Jazz represented a break from traditional music where a composer wrote an entire piece of music on paper, leaving the musicians to break their backs playing exactly what was written on the score. In a Jazz piece, however, the song is simply a starting point, or sort of a starting point for the Jazz musicians to improvise around. The song being played may have been popular and well-known that the musicians themselves did not compose, but once they had finished, the Jazz musicians had more or less written a new piece of music that bore little resemblance to the original piece. Actually, many of these early musicians were bad sight readers and some could not even read music at all. Regardless, their superb playing amazed audiences and the upbeat music they played was a different but perfect escape from the traditional music of that time.

　　How did Jazz originate? The diverse influences of the music actually reflect the American melting pot. Jazz is the cultural "mixed race" offspring of African and European-American cultures, a wondrous blend of the best elements of the two worlds. In the 1700s, slaves from Africa brought with them the songs and rhythms of their own culture, which on American soil had to be expressed through European instruments such as piano, trumpet, and saxophone. In the early part of the last century rural and urban Blacks produced a kind of synthesis of African rhythms and scales combined with Western classical harmony, resulting in such forms as "ragtime" and "blues." Through the 1920s, 1930s and 1940s Jazz rapidly developed into a complex, challenging musical art form, incorporating influences from Broadway, classical music and folk music, as well as Cuban and South American music.

　　The first Jazz is thought to have been played by African Americans and Creole musicians in New Orleans. Buddy Bolden, a cornet player, is generally considered to be the first real Jazz musician, possessing an incredible sound. Other early players of the time included Freddie Keppard, Bunk Johnson, and Clarence Williams. Most of these musicians may seem unknown to most people, but their ideas are still affecting the way Jazz is being played today. Generally these early musicians could not make very much money and worked menial jobs to make a living. The second wave of New Orleans Jazz musicians included such players as Joe Oliver, Kid Ory, and Jelly Roll Morton. These men formed small bands and took the music of earlier musicians, improved its complexity, and gained greater success.

A young cornet player by the name of Louis Armstrong was discovered by Joe Oliver in New Orleans. He soon grew to become one of the greatest and most successful musicians of all time, and later one of the biggest stars in the world. Armstrong defined what it was to play Jazz. His amazing technical abilities, the joy and spontaneity, and amazingly quick, inventive musical mind still dominate Jazz to this day. Only Charlie Parker comes close to having as much influence on the history of Jazz as Louis Armstrong did. The impact of Armstrong and other early Jazz musicians changed the way we look at music, and their work will forever be studied and admired.

Proper Names

Appalachia	n.	阿巴拉契亚(美国东部一地区)
Detroit	n.	底特律(美国密歇根州城市)
Cleveland	n.	克利夫兰(美国俄亥俄州城市)
Dallas	n.	达拉斯(美国得克萨斯州城市)
Michigan	n.	密歇根(美国州名)
Memphis	n.	孟菲斯(美国田纳西州港口城市)
Creole	n.	美国路易斯安那州的法国人后裔

For Fun

Movies to See
Walk the Line

A chronicle of country music legend Johnny Cash's life, from his early days on an Arkansas cotton farm to his rise to fame with Sun Records in Memphis, where he recorded alongside Elvis Presley, Jerry Lee Lewis and Carl Perkins.

Unit 14 The Music of America

The Legend of 1900

Though now down on his luck and disillusioned by his wartime experiences, the New Orleans-born Max was once an enthusiastic and gifted young jazz musician, and he was befriended by another young man, the pianist whose name was 1900...

Songs to Enjoy

The Beatles: **"Hey Jude"**

Hey Jude, don't make it bad, take a sad song and make it better, remember to let her into your heart, then you can start to make it better...

Simon and Garfunkel: **"The Sound of Silence"**

Hello, darkness my old friend; I've come to talk with you again because a vision softly creeping, left its seeds while I was sleeping...

Jane Monheit: **"Over the Rainbow"**

Someday I'll wish upon an star, and wake up where the clouds are far behind me, where troubles melt like lemon drops, away above the chimney tops, that's where you'll find me...

Westlife: **"The Rose"**

Some say love it is a river, that drowns the tender reed; some say love it is a razor, that leaves your soul to bleed...

Unit 15
American Literature

> There is a time in everyman's education when he arrives at the conviction that envy is ignorance; that imitation is suicide; that he must take himself for better or worse as his portion...
> —Ralph Waldo Emerson

Unit Goals

- To have a general view of American literature
- To get acquainted with some famous American writers and their works
- To recognize the typical American literary styles
- To learn some literary genres and related terms
- To develop critical thinking and intercultural communication skills
- To learn useful words and expressions concerning literature and improve English language skills

Before You Read

Test your knowledge in American literature. Match the classic lines with the works.

① "But man is not made for defeat," he said. "A man can be destroyed but not defeated."

② He was a large, broad-chested, powerfully-made man, of a full glossy black, and a face whose truly African features were characterized by an expression of grave and steady good sense, united with much kindliness and benevolence. There was something about his whole air, self-respecting and dignified, yet united with a confiding and humble simplicity.

③ There was music from my neighbor's house through the summer nights. In his blue gardens men and girls came and went like moths among the whisperings and the champagne and the stars.

④ As God is my witness, as God is my witness, they are not going to lick me. I'm going to live through this and when it's all over, I'll never be hungry again. No, nor any of my folks.

⑤ "Why didn't you dare it before?" he asked harshly. "When I hadn't a job? When I was starving?"

⑥ It was the old New York way, of taking life "without effusion of blood"; the way of people who dreaded scandal more than disease, who placed decency above courage...

_____ The Great Gatsby _____ The Age of Innocence
_____ Martin Eden _____ Gone with the Wind
_____ Uncle Tom's Cabin _____ The Old Man and the Sea

Start to Read

Text A　Overview of American Literature

1. During its early history, America was a series of British colonies on the eastern coast of the present-day United States. Therefore, its literary tradition begins as linked to the broader tradition of English Literature. However, **unique** American characteristics and the **breadth** of its production now cause it to be considered a separate path and tradition.

Early Romanticism

2. In the post-war period, with an increasing desire to produce uniquely American work, a number of key new literary figures appeared, perhaps most prominently Washington Irving (1783—1859), James Fenimore Cooper (1789—1851), and Edgar Allan Poe (1809—1849). Irving, often considered the first writer to develop a unique American style (although this is debated), wrote **humorous** works, and the well-known satire *A History of New York* (1809). In 1832, Poe began writing short stories—including "The Masque of the Red Death," "The Fall of the House of Usher," and "The Murders in the Rue Morgue"—that explored previously hidden levels of human **psychology** and pushed the boundaries of fiction toward mystery and **fantasy**. Cooper's

Leatherstocking Tales about Natty Bumppo was popular both in the new country and abroad.

3. In 1836, Ralph Waldo Emerson (1803—1882), an ex-minister, published a **startling** nonfiction work called *Nature*, in which he claimed that it was possible to **dispense** with organized religion and reach a lofty spiritual state by studying and responding to the natural world. His work influenced not only the writers who gathered around him, forming a movement known as Transcendentalism, but also the public, who heard him lecture. Emerson's most gifted fellow-thinker was perhaps Henry David Thoreau (1817—1862), a resolute nonconformist. After living mostly by himself for two years in a cabin by a wooded pond, Thoreau wrote *Walden*, a book-length memoir that urges **resistance** to the **meddlesome** dictates of organized society. His radical writings express a deep-rooted tendency toward individualism in the American character.

4. The political conflict surrounding Abolitionism inspired many writings, among which was Harriet Beecher Stowe's *Uncle Tom's Cabin*, and president Lincoln fondly **commented** her as "the little woman who wrote the book that started this great war." In 1837, the young Nathaniel Hawthorne (1804—1864) collected some of his stories as *Twice-Told Tales*, a volume rich in symbolism. Hawthorne went on to write full-length "romances" that explore such themes as guilt, pride, and emotional repression in his native New England. His **masterpiece**, *The Scarlet Letter*, is the **stark** drama of a woman cast out of her community for committing adultery.

American Lyric

5. America's two greatest 19th-century poets could hardly have been more different in **temperament** and style. Walt Whitman (1819—1892) was a working man, a traveler, a self-appointed nurse during the American Civil War, and a poetic **innovator**. His masterpiece was *Leaves of Grass*. The English novelist D. H. Lawrence wrote that Whitman "was the first to **smash** the old moral conception that the soul of man is

something superior and above the flesh."

6. Emily Dickinson (1830—1886), on the other hand, lived the sheltered life of a genteel unmarried woman in small-town. Within its formal structure, her poetry is **ingenious**, witty, and psychologically **penetrating**. Her work was **unconventional** for its day, and little of it was published during her lifetime.

Realism—Twain and James

7. Mark Twain (1835—1910) was the first major American writer to be born away from the East Coast—in the border state of Missouri. As both a writer and a humorist, Twain won a worldwide audience for his stories of youthful adventures of Tom Sawyer and Huckleberry Finn. Twain's style changed the way Americans wrote their language. Sensitive to the sound of language, he introduced **colloquial** speech into American fiction. His characters speak like real people and sound distinctively American, using local dialects, newly invented words, and regional accents. Ernest Hemingway once wrote: "All modern American literature comes from one book by Mark Twain called *Huckleberry Finn*..."

8. Henry James (1843—1916) **confronted** the Old World-New World **dilemma** by writing directly about it. Although born in New York City, he spent most of his adult years in England. Many of his novels center on Americans who live in or travel to Europe. His main **themes** were the innocence of the New World in conflict with the corruption and wisdom of the Old. Among his masterpieces is *Daisy Miller*, where the young and innocent American Daisy finds her values in conflict with European sophistication. In

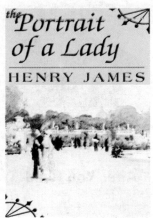

The Portrait of a Lady again a young American woman is fooled during her travels in Europe.

Turn of the 20th Century

9. At the beginning of the 20th century, American novelists were **expanding** fiction's social spectrum to **encompass** both high and low life and sometimes connected to the naturalist school of realism. In her stories and novels, Edith Wharton (1862—1937) **scrutinized** the upper-class society in which she had grown up. One of her finest books, *The Age of Innocence*, centers on a man who chooses to marry a **conventional**, socially acceptable woman rather than a fascinating outsider. At about the same time, Stephen Crane (1871—1900), best known for his Civil War novel *The Red Badge of Courage*, depicted the life of New York City prostitutes in *Maggie: A Girl of the Streets*. And in *Sister Carrie*, Theodore Dreiser (1871—1945) portrayed a country girl who moves to Chicago and becomes a kept woman.

10. American writers also expressed the disillusionment following upon the war. The stories and novels of F. Scott Fitzgerald (1896—1940) **capture** the restless, pleasure-hungry, defiant mood of the 1920s. Fitzgerald's characteristic theme, expressed **poignantly** in *The Great Gatsby*, is the tendency of youth's golden dreams to **dissolve** in failure and disappointment. Ernest Hemingway (1899—1961) saw violence and death first-hand as an ambulance driver in World War I, and the **carnage** persuaded him that abstract language was mostly empty and misleading. He cut out unnecessary words from his  writing, simplified the sentence structure, and concentrated on **concrete** objects and actions. He **adhered** to a moral code that emphasized grace under pressure, and his **protagonists** were strong, silent men who often dealt awkwardly with women. *The Sun Also Rises* and *A Farewell to Arms* are generally considered his best novels; in 1954, he won the Nobel Prize in Literature.

After You Read

Knowledge Focus

1. Consider the following questions.
    1) What are the major differences between Romanticism and Realism?
    2) What are the features of Transcendentalism?
    3) What is the significance of the novel *Uncle Tom's Cabin*?

2. Match the writers with their works.
    ① Walt Whitman   ② Harriet Beecher Stowe
    ③ Jack London   ④ Mark Twain
    ⑤ Nathaniel Hawthorne ⑥ Ernest Hemingway

⑦ Margaret Mitchell   ⑧ O Henry
⑨ Henry James   ⑩ Edith Wharton

_____ "The Gift of the Magi"   _____ The Scarlet Letter
_____ The Call of the Wild   _____ A Farewell to Arms
_____ Leaves of Grass   _____ Adventures of Tom Sawyer
_____ Uncle Tom's Cabin   _____ Gone with the Wind
_____ The Age of Innocence   _____ The Portrait of a Lady

3. Summarize the writing features of the following writers in your own words.
   1) Edgar Allan Poe _____
   2) Henry David Thoreau _____
   3) Nathaniel Hawthorne _____
   4) Walt Whitman _____
   5) Emily Dickinson _____
   6) Mark Twain _____
   7) Henry James _____
   8) Ernest Hemingway _____

Language Focus

1. Complete the following sentences with the proper words and expressions listed below.

unique	prominent	dispense with	theme
cast out of	temperament	conventional	defiant
adhere to	encompass	dilemma	in conflict with

   1) Since we know each other so well, let's _____ formalities.
   2) In the eternal universe, every one has only one chance to live, and therefore everyone's existence is _____.
   3) Racial harmony should _____ three main factors: mutual respect, social harmony, and public security.
   4) The twin sisters are so alike in appearance, but completely different in _____.
   5) Self-identity is a common _____ of African-American literary works.
   6) Our Party should _____ the policy of reform and opening to the outside.
   7) The playwrights broke out of the old _____ straitjacket.
   8) She was in a(n) _____ as to whether to stay at school or to get a job.
   9) He is a(n) _____ scholar in the field of linguistics.
   10) Science is _____ religion.
   11) The parents showed remarkable forbearance to their _____ and unruly son.
   12) After the scandal, he is _____ the company.

2. **Fill in each blank with a suitable preposition or adverb.**

   1) In the post-war period, _____ an increasing desire to produce uniquely American work, a number of key new literary figures appeared.

   2) In *Nature*, Ralph Waldo Emerson claimed that it was possible to dispense _____ organized religion and reach a lofty spiritual state by studying and responding to the natural world.

   3) Thoreau wrote *Walden*, a book-length memoir that urges resistance _____ the meddlesome dictates of organized society.

   4) Sensitive _____ the sound of language, Mark Twain introduced colloquial speech into American fiction.

   5) Henry James' main themes were the innocence of the New World _____ conflict _____ corruption and wisdom of the Old.

   6) Ernest Hemingway adhered _____ a moral code that emphasized grace under pressure, and his protagonists were strong, silent men who often dealt awkwardly with women.

3. **Proofreading and error correction.**

   The passage contains FIVE errors. Each indicated line contains a maximum of ONE error. In each case, only ONE word is involved.

The decisions about whether and how to generalize about the study of minority literature is complex because the history of minorities in the U. S. and the academic study of their literatures and cultures. African American contributions to the literature and culture of the U. S. are older than the Republic; moreover, academic institutionalization of their study came more recently emerging with the Civil Rights movement in the 1960s. Interest and study of the cultural production of other people of color followed, but if and how they are analogous remains a topic of debate.	1) _____ 2) _____ 3) _____ 4) _____ 5) _____

Comprehensive Work

1. **Share ideas with your group members.**

   Work in groups. Discuss with your partners about the meanings of the following quotes on books. Do you agree with the speakers?

   1) The books that the world calls immoral are books that show the world its own shame.

   　　　　　　　　　　　　　　　　　　　　　　—Oscar Wilde

2) The man who does not read good books has no advantage over the man who cannot read them.

—Mark Twain

3) Next to acquiring good friends, the best acquisition is that of good books.

—Charles Caleb Colton

4) Books are divided into two classes, the books of the hour and the books of all time.

—John Ruskin

5) A good novel tells us the truth about its hero; but a bad novel tells us the truth about its author.

—Gilbert Keith Chesterton

2. **Essay Writing.**

What do you think can people benefit from reading literary works?

Read More

Text B   Man Is Not Made for Defeat

There were no such lines. There was only the heavy sharp blue head and the big eyes and the clicking, thrusting all-swallowing jaws.

But that was the location of the brain and the old man hit it. He hit it with his blood mushed hands driving a good harpoon with all his strength. He hit it without hope but with resolution and complete malignancy.

The shark swung over and the old man saw his eye was not alive and then he swung over once again, wrapping himself in two loops of the rope.

The old man knew that he was dead but the shark would not accept it. Then, on his back, with his tail lashing and his jaws clicking, the shark plowed over the water as a speedboat does.

The water was white where his tail beat it and three-quarters of his body was clear above the water when the rope came taut, shivered, and then snapped. The shark lay quietly for a little while on the surface and the old man watched him. Then he went down very slowly.

"He took about forty pounds," the old man said aloud. He took my harpoon too and all the rope, he thought, and now my fish bleeds again and there will be others.

He did not like to look at the fish anymore since he had been mutilated. When the fish had been hit it was as though he himself were hit.

But I killed the shark that hit my fish, he thought. And he was the biggest dentuso that I have ever seen. And God knows that I have seen big ones.

It was too good to last, he thought. I wish it had been a dream now and that I had never hooked the fish and was alone in bed on the newspapers.

"But man is not made for defeat," he said. "A man can be destroyed but not defeated." I am sorry that I killed the fish though, he thought. Now the bad time is coming and I do not even have the harpoon. The dentuso is cruel and able and strong and intelligent. But I was more intelligent than he was. Perhaps not, he thought. Perhaps I was only better armed.

"Don't think, old man," he said aloud. "Sail on this course and take it when it comes."

But I must think, he thought. Because it is all I have left. That and baseball. I wonder how the great DiMaggio would have liked the way I hit him in the brain? It was no great thing, he thought. Any man could do it. But do you think my hands were as great a handicap as the bone spurs? I cannot know. I never had anything wrong with my heel except the time the sting ray stung it when I stepped on him when swimming and paralyzed the lower leg and made the unbearable pain.

"Think about something cheerful, old man," he said. "Every minute now you are closer to home. You sail lighter for the loss of forty pounds."

He knew quite well the pattern of what could happen when he reached the inner part of the current. But there was nothing to be done now.

"Yes, there is," he said aloud. "I can lash my knife to the butt of one of the oars." So he did that with the tiller under his arm and the sheet of the sail under his foot.

"Now," he said. "I am still an old man. But I am not unarmed."

The breeze was fresh now and he sailed on well. He watched only the forward part of the fish and some of his hope returned.

It is silly not to hope, he thought.

Finish the following exercises.

1. The passage is from the work _____, and the author of the work is _____.
2. In the novel, the author emphasized "grace under pressure"; the real hero is one that "can be _____ but not _____."
3. According to the description, the readers know that the scene is on _____.
4. In the passage, the author depicts a fierce fight between _____ and _____.

Text C   The Tempest

(from *Adventures of Tom Sawyer*)

There was a brooding oppressiveness in the air that seemed to bode something. The boys huddled themselves together and sought the friendly companionship of the fire, though the dull dead heat of the breathless atmosphere was stifling. They sat still, intent and waiting. The solemn hush continued. Beyond the light of the fire everything was swallowed up in the blackness of darkness. Presently there came a quivering glow that vaguely revealed the foliage for a moment and then vanished. By and by another came, a little stronger. Then another. Then a faint moan came sighing through the branches of the forest and the boys felt a fleeting breath upon their cheeks, and shuddered with the fancy that the Spirit of the Night had gone by. There was a pause. Now a weird flash turned night into day and showed every little grass-blade, separate and distinct, that grew about their feet. And it showed three white, startled faces, too. A deep peal of thunder went rolling and tumbling down the heavens and lost itself in sullen rumblings in the distance. A sweep of chilly air passed by, rustling all the leaves and snowing the flaky ashes broadcast about the fire. Another fierce glare lit up the forest and an instant crash followed that seemed to rend the tree-tops right over the boys' heads. They clung together in terror, in the thick gloom that followed. A few big rain-drops fell pattering upon the leaves.

"Quick! boys, go for the tent!" exclaimed Tom.

They sprang away, stumbling over roots and among vines in the dark, no two plunging in the same direction. A furious blast roared through the trees, making everything sing as it went. One blinding flash after another came, and peal on peal of deafening thunder. And now a drenching rain poured down and the rising hurricane drove it in sheets along the ground. The boys cried out to each other, but the roaring wind and the booming thunder-blasts drowned their voices utterly. However, one by one they straggled in at last and took shelter under the tent, cold, scared, and streaming with water; but to have company in misery seemed something to be grateful for. They could not talk, the old sail flapped so furiously, even if the other noises would have allowed them. The tempest rose higher and higher, and presently the sail tore loose from its fastenings and went winging away on the blast. The boys seized each others' hands and fled, with many tumblings and bruises, to the shelter of a great oak that stood upon the river-bank. Now the battle was at its highest. Under the ceaseless conflagration of lightning that flamed in the skies, everything below stood out in clean-cut and shadowless distinctness: the bending trees, the billowy river, white with foam, the driving spray of spume-flakes, the dim outlines of the high bluffs on the other side, glimpsed through the drifting cloud-rack and the slanting veil of rain. Every little while some giant tree yielded the fight and fell crashing through the younger growth; and the unflagging thunder-peals came now in ear-splitting explosive bursts, keen and sharp, and unspeakably appalling. The storm culminated in one matchless effort that seemed likely to tear the island to pieces, burn it up, drown it to the tree-tops, blow it away, and deafen every creature in it, all at one and the same moment. It was a wild night for homeless young heads to be out in.

But at last the battle was done, and the forces retired with weaker and weaker threatenings and grumblings, and peace resumed her sway.

Finish the following exercises.

1. The passage is from *Adventures of Tom Sawyer*. The author of the novel is _____.
2. "Now a weird flash turned night into day and showed every little grass-blade, separate and distinct, that grew about their feet." Here the "weird flash" refers to the _____.
3. Word Partners: Please match the adjectives with their proper noun partners.

drenching	river
chilly	glare
deafening	rain
billowy	thunder
blinding	air

4. All of the following words are of similar meanings except _____.

    a. storm   b. hurricane   c. tempest   d. blizzard

Text D   How to Read Stories

The first piece of advice we would like to give you for reading a story is this: Read it quickly and with total immersion. Ideally, a story should be read at one sitting, although this is rarely possible for busy people with long novels. Nevertheless, the ideal should be approximated by compressing the reading of a good story into as short a time as feasible. Otherwise you will forget what happened, the unity of the plot will escape you, and you will be lost.

Some readers, when they really like a novel, want to savor it, to pause over it, to draw out the reading of it for as long as they can. But in this case they are probably not so much reading the book as satisfying their more or less unconscious feelings about the events and the characters. We will return to that in a moment.

Read quickly, we suggest, and with total immersion. We have indicated the importance of letting an imaginative book work on you. That is what we mean by the latter phrase. Let the characters into your mind and heart; suspend your disbelief, if such it is, about the events. Do not disapprove of something a character does before you understand why he does it—if then. Try as hard as you can to live in his world, not in yours; there, the things he does may be quite understandable. And do not judge the world as a whole until you are sure that you have "lived" in it to the extent of your ability.

Following this rule will allow you to answer the first question you should ask about any book—What is it about, as a whole? Unless you read it quickly you will fail to see the unity of the story. Unless you read intensely you will fail to see the details.

The terms of a story, as we have observed, are its characters and incidents. You must become acquainted with them, and be able to sort them out. But here a word of warning. To take *War and Peace* as an example, many readers start this great novel and are overwhelmed by the vast number of characters to whom they are introduced, especially since they all have strange-sounding names. They soon give up on the book in the belief that they will never be able to sort out all the complicated relationships, to know who is who. This is true of any big novel—and if a novel is really good, we want it to be as big as possible.

It does not always occur to such fainthearted readers that exactly the same thing happens to them when they move to a new town or part of a town, when they go to a new school or job, or even when they arrive at a party. They do not give up in those circumstances; they know that after a short while individuals will begin to be visible in the mass, friends will emerge from the faceless crowd of fellow-workers, fellow-students, or fellow-guests. We may not remember the names of everyone we met at a party, but we will recall the name of the man we talked to for an hour, or the girl with whom we made a date for the next evening, or the mother whose child goes to the same school as ours. The same thing happens in a novel. We should not expect to remember every character; many of them are merely background persons, who are there only to set off the actions of the main characters. However, by the time we have finished *War and Peace* or any big novel, we know who is important, and we do not forget. Pierre, Andrew, Natasha, Princess Mary, Nicholas—the names are likely to come immediately to memory, although it may have been years since we read Tolstoy's book.

We also, despite the plethora of incidents, soon learn *what* is important. Authors generally give a good deal of help in this respect; they do not want the reader to miss what is essential to the unfolding of the plot, so they flag it in various ways. But our point is that you should not be anxious if all is not clear from the beginning. Actually, it should *not* be clear then. A story is like life itself; in life, we do not expect to understand events as they occur, at least with total clarity, but looking back on them, we do understand. So the reader of a story, looking back on it after he has finished it, understands the relation of events and the order of actions.

All of this comes down to the same point: you must finish a story in order to be able to say that you have read it well. Paradoxically, however, a story ceases to be like life on its last page. Life goes on, but the story does not. Its characters have no vitality outside the book, and your imagination of what happens to them before the first page and after the last is only as good as the next reader's. Actually, all such speculations are meaningless. Preludes to *Hamlet* have been written, but they are ridiculous. We should not ask what happens to Pierre and Natasha after *War and Peace* ends. We are satisfied with

Shakespeare's and Tolstoy's creations partly because they are limited in time. We need no more.

The great majority of books that are read are stories of one kind or another. People who cannot read listen to stories. We even make them up for ourselves. Fiction seems to be a necessity for human beings. Why is this?

One reason why fiction is a human necessity is that it satisfies many unconscious as well as conscious needs. It would be important if it only touched the conscious mind, as expository writing does. But fiction is important, too, because it also touches the unconscious.

On the simplest level—and a discussion of this subject could be very complex—we like or dislike certain kinds of people more than others, without always being sure why. If, in a novel, such people are rewarded or punished, we may have stronger feelings, either pro or con, about the book than it merits artistically.

For example, we are often pleased when a character in a novel inherits money, or otherwise comes into good fortune. However, this tends to be true only if the character is "sympathetic"—meaning that we can identify with him or her. We do not admit to ourselves that we would like to inherit the money, we merely say that we like the book.

Perhaps we would all like to love more richly than we do. Many novels are about love—most are, perhaps—and it gives us pleasure to identify with the loving characters. They are free, and we are not. But we may not want to admit this; for to do so might make us feel, consciously, that our own loves are inadequate.

Again, almost everyone has some unconscious sadism and masochism in his makeup. These are often satisfied in novels, where we can identify with either the conqueror or victim, or even with both. In each case, we are prone to say simply that we like "that kind of book"—without specifying or really knowing why.

Finally, we suspect that life as we know it is unjust. Why do good people suffer, and bad ones prosper? We do not know, we cannot know, but the fact causes great anxiety in everyone. In stories, this chaotic and unpleasant situation is adjusted, and that is extremely satisfying to us.

In stories—in novels and narrative poems and plays justice usually does exist. People get what they deserve; the author, who is like a god to his characters, sees to it that they are rewarded or punished according to their true merit. In a good story, in a satisfying one, this is usually so, at least. One of the most irritating things about a bad story is that the people in it seem to be punished or rewarded with no rhyme or reason. The great storyteller makes no mistakes. He is able to convince us that justice—poetic justice, we call it—has been done.

This is true even of high tragedy. There, terrible things happen to good men, but we see that the hero, even if he does not wholly deserve his fate, at least comes to understand it. And we have a profound desire to share his understanding. If we only *knew*—then we could withstand whatever the world has in store for us. "I Want to Know Why" is the title of a story by Sherwood Anderson. It could be the title of many stories. The tragic hero does learn why, though often, of course, only after the ruin of his life. We can share his insight without sharing his suffering.

Thus, in criticizing fiction we must be careful to distinguish those books that satisfy our own particular unconscious needs—the ones that make us say, "I like this book, although I don't really know why"—from those that satisfy the deep unconscious needs of almost everybody. The latter are undoubtedly the great stories, the ones that live on and on for generations and centuries. As long as man is man, they will go on satisfying him, giving him something that he needs to have—a belief in justice and understanding and the allaying of anxiety. We do not know, we cannot be sure, that the real world is good. But the world of a great story is somehow good. We want to live there as often and as long as we can.

Finish the exercises.
1. The first piece of advice on how to read a story is to _____.
2. By "total immersion," we mean to _____.
3. If you read a story very slowly, you will _____.
4. It does not always occur to such fainthearted readers that exactly the same thing happens to them when they move to a new town or part of a town, when they go to a new school or job, or even when they arrive at a party. "The same thing" refers to _____.
5. How is a story similar to or different from life?
6. Fiction seems to be a necessity for human beings. Why?
7. One of the most irritating things about a bad story is that _____.

For Fun

Books to Read

Jack London: *The Call of the Wild*

A dog named Buck is stolen from his home in the Santa Clara Valley of California, and taken to the Alaskan gold fields to be a sled dog.

Mark Twain: *Adventures of Tom Sawyer*

Tom and Huck went hunting for buried treasure and witnessed something terrible...

Movies to See

Gone with the Wind

A dark-haired, green-eyed Georgia belle struggles through the hardships of the Civil War and Reconstruction.

A Streetcar Named Desire

Disturbed Blanche DuBois moves in with her sister in New Orleans and is tormented by her brutish brother-in-law while her reality crumbles around her.

重点参考书目和网站

［1］Bloom. A (1987). *The Closing of the American Mind*. New York：Simon & Schuster Inc.

［2］Bremer，F. J. (2009). *Puritanism：A Very Short Introduction*. Oxford：Oxford University Press.

［3］Brogan，D. W. (1944). *The American Character*. New York：Alfred A. Knopf.

［4］Counts，G. S. (1962). *Education and the Foundations of Human Freedom*. Pittsburgh：University of Pittsburgh Press.

［5］Cullen，J. (2003). *The American Dream：A Short History of an Idea That Shaped a Nation*. Oxford：Oxford University Press.

［6］Davis，F. (1992). *Fashion，Culture，and Identity*. Chicago：University of Chicago Press.

［7］Handlin，O. (1957). *Race and Nationality in American Life*. Boston：Little，Brown.

［8］Hutchins，R. M. (1936). *The Higher Learning in America*. New Haven：Yale University Press.

［9］Kennedy，J. F. (1964). *A Nation of Immigrants*. New York：Harper & Row.

［10］Lowi，T. and Benjamin Ginsberg (1994). *American Government：Freedom and Power*. New York：W. W. Norton.

［11］McDonogh，G. W.，Robert Gregg & Cindy H. Wong. Eds.（2000）*Encyclopedia of Contemporary American Culture*. New York：Routledge.

［12］Ritchie，D. A. (2010). *The U. S. Congress：A Very Short Introduction*. Oxford：Oxford University Press.

［13］Scanzoni，J. H. (1975). *Sex Roles，Life Styles，and Childbearing：Changing Patterns in Marriage and the Family*. New York：Free Press.

［14］Broukal，M.，Janet Milhomme. (2003) 美国文化一览——再看美国［M］. 济南：山东科学技术出版社.

［15］埃塞尔·蒂尔斯基、马丁·蒂尔斯基编著.（2006）美国制度与文化（引进版）［M］. 北京：中国人民大学出版社.

［16］池小泉主编.（2007）西方文化风情路——美国篇［M］. 西安：西北工业大学出版社.

［17］姜志伟、罗德喜、李啸主编.（2004）大学英语——英美文化链接（中英双语本）［M］. 北京：中国书籍出版社.

［18］刘晓菓主编.（2005）英语国家社会与文化（上册）［M］. 北京：中国电力出版社.

［19］刘晓菓主编.（2005）英语国家社会与文化（下册）［M］. 北京：中国电力出版社.

［20］玛丽安娜·卡尼·戴特斯曼、乔安·克兰德尔、爱德华·N.卡尼.（2006）美国文化背景（第3版）［M］. 陈国华译. 北京：世界图书出版公司北京公司.

［21］钱清编译.（2006）礼仪与风俗（英汉对照）［M］. 北京：外文出版社.

［22］王纯才编.（2006）美国［M］. 南京：江苏文艺出版社.

［23］王恩铭编.（2003）美国文化与社会［M］. 上海：上海外语教育出版社.

［24］汪榕培、任秀桦主编.（1996）英语学习背景知识词典［M］. 上海：上海外语教育出版社.

［25］周静琼编著.（2003）当代美国概况［M］. 上海：上海外语教育出版社.

［26］朱永涛编著.（1991）英美文化基础教程［M］. 北京：外语教学与研究出版社.

［27］朱永涛、王立礼主编.（2005）英语国家社会与文化入门·上册（第二版）［M］. 北京：高等教育出版社.

[28] 朱永涛、王立礼主编.(2005)英语国家社会与文化入门·下册(第二版)[M].北京:高等教育出版社.

[29] 朱昱、代芊编译.(2006)节日与婚礼(英汉对照)[M].北京:外文出版社.

[30] 朱振武主编,白岸杨、江先发编著.(2006)英语夜读15分钟·经典[Z].上海:上海译文出版社.

[31] 朱振武主编,张柯、陈慧莲编著.(2006)英语夜读15分钟·时文[Z].上海:上海译文出版社.

[32] 朱振武主编,赵永健、信艳编著.(2006)英语夜读15分钟·文化[Z].上海:上海译文出版社.

[33] Culture of the United States:http://en.wikipedia.org/wiki/Culture_of_the_United_States, accessed Mar.29,2021.

[34] Federal Government of the United States:http://en.wikipedia.org/wiki/U.S._government, accessed Mar.29,2021.

[35] Life in the USA:American Culture:http://www.lifeintheusa.com/culture/index.html, accessed Mar.29,2021.

[36] Music of the United States:http://en.wikipedia.org/wiki/Music_of_the_United_States, accessed Mar.29,2021.

[37] Muzikum:http://muzikum.eu, accessed Mar.29,2021.

[38] Religion in the United States:http://en.wikipedia.org/wiki/Religion_in_the_United_States, accessed Mar.29,2021.

[39] Sports in the United States:http://en.wikipedia.org/wiki/Sports_in_the_United_States, accessed Mar.29,2021.

[40] U.S. Federal Government:http://www.usagov.com/Agencies/federal.shtml, accessed Mar.29,2021.

美国国情：美国社会与文化（第3版）

尊敬的老师：

　　您好！

　　本书练习题配有参考答案，请联系责任编辑索取。同时，为了方便您更好地使用本教材，获得最佳教学效果，我们特向使用该书作为教材的教师赠送本教材配套电子资料。如有需要，请完整填写"教师联系表"并加盖所在单位系（院）公章，免费向出版社索取。

北京大学出版社

教 师 联 系 表

教材名称	美国国情：美国社会与文化（第3版）			
姓名：	性别：	职务：		职称：
E-mail：	联系电话：		邮政编码：	
供职学校：		所在院系：		（章）
学校地址：				
教学科目与年级：		班级人数：		
通信地址：				

　　填写完毕后，请将此表邮寄给我们，我们将为您免费寄送本教材配套资料，谢谢！

北京市海淀区成府路 205 号
北京大学出版社外语编辑部　　吴宇森　　　外语编辑部电话：010-62759634
邮政编码：100871　　　　　　　　　　　　邮　购　部　电　话：010-62534449
电子邮箱：wuyusen@pup.cn　　　　　　　　市场营销部电话：010-62750672